Sugar Cravings Conquered

Break Free from Your Sugar Addiction

Olivia Rivers

Exclusive Bonus: Ignite Your Sugar-Free Journey!

"Crush Sugar Cravings: Your Ultimate Detox Roadmap" is your essential guide to reclaiming control over your health by breaking free from the hold of sugar cravings. Empower yourself with practical strategies, delicious recipes, and unwavering support on your journey to conquer sugar addiction.

How This Book Can Help You:

This empowering eBook provides you with the tools and guidance necessary to embrace a life free from the grip of sugar addiction. Each page is a testament to your commitment to well-being, offering practical strategies, nourishing recipes, and unwavering support. By incorporating the wisdom and insights from *"Crush Sugar Cravings"* into your life, you are embarking on a transformative journey toward radiant health and an empowered relationship with food.

With this exclusive bonus, you're taking the first bold step towards the vibrant, energized life you deserve.

Scan the QR code to unlock your complimentary guide and step into a life liberated from sugar's sway.

Table of Contents

Introduction

It really is true that all the great things in life are super bad for us.

Just think of all those great parties we may have gone to when we were young. For me, it was those big college keg parties, where you would pay 10 dollars at the door and get however much of the keg you wanted. By the end of the night, most people had drunk their body weight in beer, and someone had tried jumping off the roof and into the pool. More than a few times a couple of aggressive fellas duked it out over a girl neither of them had a chance with. Each of these events was, at the time, among the most fun I have ever had.

But as an adult, I see now how unhealthy the whole thing was. Just the beer alone—and not just the calories, either. What was it doing to my brain?

The person who jumped off the roof was lucky they didn't die. But statistically speaking, I feel like they should have at least broken something. And fistfights have more than once gotten out of hand and ended in someone getting hurt for real. So, none of that, on the whole, was advisable.

Now, would I trade those memories for the world? Of course not. But I am older and wiser now, and know better than to do things like that. Ultimately, I can chalk it all up to experience and move on to better things.

Unfortunately, that rule I started this off with still remains: The best things in life tend to be super bad for us. All the things we enjoy and take for granted? Most of them have a dark underbelly to them. We have to have defenses lined up against these things, lest they get the better of us.

One of these things—in fact, maybe the most common—is sugar.

Now, before we get started, I am not here to give you a bunch of keto-related points we have all heard a billion times by now. The keto diet makes a horrific mistake in assuming that natural sugars are bad for you when, on the contrary, they are more than just a little essential. In fact, sugar—in the form of carbs—is what gives us the energy we need to live.

Instead, I am here to talk about sugar of a different stripe, the unhealthy kind. The kind we find in sodas, candy, and so on. The kind, as it turns out, that some people can develop a problematic—some would even say *addictive*—relationship with.

Let's start with some definitions to get things moving. Natural sugars are those found in whole foods. They are in fruits, whole grain breads, vegetables, meat, dairy, the works. "Refined" sugars, meanwhile, often come from natural sources, but all the other stuff you get from whole foods has been taken out. All that is left is the sugar, which becomes problematic when isolated, plus a whole bunch of other junk like preservatives.

And it is these that cause issues with people. But while we already know about things like diabetes and the like, the subject here is specifically sugar *addiction* and the problems that run downstream from this behavior.

So, the next logical question is—can we actually get addicted to refined sugar?

Well, let me tell you a story. When I was in elementary school, there was a boy named Ralph. He was from one of those families that seemed to be genetically predisposed to obesity, but every time you went over to his house and saw how they ate, it was pretty clear there was some free will involved in this predicament.

Not that I am picking on them, you understand. I am just illustrating that Ralph did not really have much of a chance, given his environment.

With that in mind, though, it made sense that he was often seen nursing a soda, even as a young boy. Heck, his mom packed him a can of Coke every day for his lunch. At the time, I thought that was pretty cool, of course. I even asked my mom how come I didn't get soda for lunch.

She told me matter-of-factly that it was viciously unhealthy, but I didn't understand that. At least, not at the time. As an adult, I totally get it now.

See, what happened with Ralph was, by the time he was in sixth grade, he was bringing more than just a can for every lunch. At some point, although I am not sure when, there was a *second* can of Coke. Then a *third*. By the time he got to the eighth grade, he had a whopping *four cans of Coke every lunch*.

Now, kids being kids, he obviously got teased about how much Coke he drank. And I'd like to say he took it in his stride, but that was a lot of caffeine and sugar for a young guy. When he was pushed around, he would lash out like a wolverine and attack the first person who laughed at him.

After a few detentions for fighting at recess, Ralph's parents were brought in and told that Ralph was being violent at school. The principal even said she was sure the caffeine and sugar were responsible for this. And, furthermore, she was worried about the toll such a habit was taking on the boy's health.

In the years since then, I have been told that Ralph's parents took this as a personal attack and lashed out at the principal. Their approach was along the lines of, "How dare you question our parenting"—that sort of thing.

In any case, the intervention didn't work. Ralph continued to drink four cans of Coke at lunch, plus—he told me later—three he had for breakfast, and an additional five between the time he got home and went to sleep. Sleep was becoming an issue for Ralph, since, as you can imagine, he was quite wired.

And more than that, he was really ballooning, weight-wise. Even for a young guy, his weight was quite out of control. But, of course, he kept on drinking his Coke as though nothing was the matter.

This lasted well into high school, which was when a doctor finally put his foot down and said this much soda was not good for the kid. "Look," the doctor said, "the poor boy's not even sleeping. He looks exhausted."

And it is at this point that the story becomes interesting for us. Because up until now, I could understand many of you saying, "Well, Coke has caffeine, as you said. That's what's got him addicted."

And you know what? You're probably right. His parents had to wean him off the Coke, which was, by all accounts, quite the ordeal. But eventually, he kicked his cola habit, down from a dozen a day to precisely *zero*.

At least, zero *Cokes* a day. Because, like many addicts, he substituted one thing for another. And the other was good ol' non-caffeinated soda of an orange flavor.

I know, I know. Who the heck drinks orange sodas? Well, Ralph did. He drank those things until he got up to a habit of 12 or more a day. He put on ridiculous amounts of weight, constantly had a headache, and, what is worse, lost most of his teeth.

Yeah. His teeth. As I said, most of them are gone. But the ones that are left?

God help him.

To this day, Ralph is notorious in town for his soda drinking. He never goes outside without one. He orders insane quantities of the stuff when he goes to the movies.

And never, in keeping with his first time kicking the habit, does he drink anything with caffeine. Again, he's all about the non-caffeinated stuff now.

What will the consequences of this habit be? Well, they could be a few things. Diabetes is certainly coming, if it hasn't already arrived. And I already mentioned his teeth. But there is a good to fair chance that he is staring down the barrel of some very serious medical problems unless he stops drinking all those gosh darn sodas.

Kind of a silly problem on its surface, isn't it? Some people are addicted to *heroin*, for crying out loud. And Ralph is addicted to soda?

Well, as we go through this book, we are going to learn that this sugar addiction phenomenon is no laughing matter. It is real, it is harmful, and it is horrifyingly pervasive. And if you, dear reader, are currently in the throes of a sugar addiction, then I hope this book can also offer a few solutions to this problem.

So, without further ado, what say we get moving here? We have a lot of ground to cover. A lot of sources to consult. And only so long to do it.

Let's get started.

Chapter 1:

Understanding Sugar

Addiction

One of the challenging things about sugar is that we really do, as people, love it. And there are reasons for this that we will get into in a moment, but for now, suffice it to say, sugar is one of our great loves.

Don't believe me? Just think of all the things we add it to. Our coffee, for example. Every morning, an enormous number of people have a coffee to wake up. And for many of those people, the bitter taste of the great drink in its blackened state is not enough. Nor, it seems, is the effect of the caffeine. So, we add sugar to it.

And as if the teaspoons of sugar we add were not enough, just think of all the crazy sugary coffee drinks we ingest on a regular basis. The ones with the caramel-infused this or that, the mochas, the lattes and cappuccinos, the iced sugar cold shaken things... The list goes on.

Sugar, in other words, is a total mainstay of the Western diet. But it is also not classically addictive, at least not in the sense that we use that word normally. When we talk about something being addictive, we usually mean something like alcohol or cocaine. Sugar, it seems, is outside of the realm of addictive substances.

But is that true? Or is there something deeper at work here? Is there, perhaps, a part of our neurochemistry that supports the idea of sugar being addictive?

Or, put another way: *Just what the heck is a sugar addiction, anyway?*

The Science of Addiction

So, addiction is a complicated matter that is influenced by a whole variety of factors, both environmental and genetic. We all know, for example, about the so-called "addictive personality," which is the person who, much as they might try otherwise, winds up easily addicted to substances, activities, or both.

But if we zero in on the biology—or, more specifically, the neurochemistry—of addiction, we find that there is one influence that stands above all as the force behind it. And that is the influence of the neurotransmitter dopamine.

Put in the simplest terms possible, dopamine is the chemical responsible for giving you pleasure and satisfaction at having completed a task. It is released when you exercise, have sex, do drugs, read a book, make someone laugh—basically, it is working and active all the time.

How it works, is that when you do something "good," dopamine is released to signal that this was a pleasurable experience. It then converts that pleasurable experience into a memory, both as a memory of the thing itself, i.e., the activity that was pleasurable, but also as a procedural memory, meaning you remember what you need to do to repeat that activity.

So, say you are learning to play the guitar. When you first start playing, just getting a decent sound out of the instrument is almost impossible. It clicks because you can't press down on the strings hard enough; the pick slips from your hand or goes sideways; you press down on the wrong fret. The early stages of learning this instrument are, in a nutshell, an utter mess.

But if you work at it long enough, eventually you will get a good sound out of it. You have the pick in the proper position, your finger on the right fret, and you are pushing down hard enough that you get a nice, clean, ringing sound. Once this happens, you feel a sense of reward: You have worked at something with a goal in mind, and it has paid off.

So, right there is the first sign of dopamine. You did the thing you were trying to do, which made you feel good. But all this would be for naught if you had to start from scratch every time you picked up the guitar. This is why dopamine converts this process into a memory—so that the next time you try and make a clean, ringing sound on that guitar, it will be easier to do. The distance between your goal and your ability shrinks in order to maximize the potential for pleasure. And what is maybe most important, this whole process tells you *that you should return to this activity in order to feel that pleasure again.*

The trick with dopamine, though, is that while it is absolutely essential for our being able to function, it also has its dark side. Because, as I am sure you can see by now, this circuit of performing a task, feeling pleasure because of it, and then turning it into a memory so that you both want to return to the task *and* know how to pull it off more easily than before, is exactly the circuit of addiction.

We can see this more easily if we tell the story of learning to play the guitar again, except that this time, it is about alcohol. In this version, we drink beer, which produces a kind of "high"—a sense of relaxation and euphoria. "Pleasure," in other words. Our brain tells us that this is a good thing, remembers that beer is the source of pleasure, and then further converts this into a memory about how to obtain (i.e., drink) beer, in order to repeat this experience. And, most importantly, it tells you that you should return to this activity again in order to repeat the pleasurable experience.

If this process gets out of hand, and we return to, say, beer, over and over again, for that sense of pleasure, then we can become so consumed by our pursuit of the alcohol-induced pleasure that we become dependent on it. Thus, addiction.

But, of course, this book is not about alcohol addiction. It is about sugar addiction. So: Given dopamine's influence and the circuit of reward, can we become addicted to sugar?

The answer is obviously "Yes." Because not only does sugar activate the dopamine pathway, but it activates our opiate receptors as well (Schaefer & Yasin, 2023).

Which, by the way, blew my mind when I first read that. "For real?" I said. "The opiate pathways?" But, yes, this is apparently true. And it is for this reason that some researchers suggest that sugar may be more addictive than even cocaine.

Not that this is without controversy, understand. Of course, there are researchers who disagree with this. But consider that people who develop a habit of eating sweets will often continue to do so no matter the ramifications to their health. That means all the weight gain, the diabetes, the headaches, and even the hormonal imbalances—these are still fair game. What other than a severe addiction explains why someone would continue to do something even as it is killing them?

In fact, at least one study on rats has found that sugar activates more neurons located in their pleasure centers than cocaine does. And their behavior upon developing the habit was exactly what you would expect from an addict: They start with cravings, they go on a binge, and then they begin to go through withdrawal.

Interestingly, the study on rats was done with Oreo cookies. And the rats also ate the filling first. So, say what you will about the inapplicability of rat testing to humans, we really, as horrifying as it may sound, are not that unlike rats.

So, where the disagreement among researchers comes in is twofold: To begin with, declaring food products to be addictive is challenging because food is necessary for survival. Amphetamines, for example, are not. But also, with sugar, there is disagreement on, at the very least, the *extent* to which it is addictive—namely, whether the attention-getting headline "More Addictive Than Cocaine" is accurate.

Where there is broad agreement, however, is that sugar stimulates the regions of the brain classically associated with addiction and leads to identical behaviors. Now, I am not a doctor. But if it looks like a duck, and it quacks like a duck...?

Anyway, the point here is that whether sugar is addictive in a strict, clinical sense, or if it just leads to the same results, sugar can at least lead to you being a kind of pseudo-addict, which comes with a whole host of health complications you should want to stay as far away from as possible.

It is those complications we are going to get into here in a second. But first, maybe we should take a brief step back and clear up which kind of sugars we are talking about here. Because, as it turns out, not all sugars are created equal.

What Kind of Sugar Are We Talking about Here?

So, I mentioned earlier that we are not going to do some keto thing about how all sugars, especially carbs, should be avoided. And that is true—we're not. But even saying that we are dealing with specifically "refined" sugar does not *necessarily* narrow down our focus.

Because there still remains the question of what exactly is meant by refined sugar. It is one of those terms, I think, which is used a lot, and which everyone has heard, but whose meaning remains, for most of us, elusive.

Starting from there then, refined sugar is generally either table sugar or high-fructose corn syrup. Table sugar starts its life in sugar cane or sugar beets. In other words, its origin is perfectly natural. How the sugars which occur naturally in those plants become refined, is that their juices are extracted by putting them in hot water, and those juices are turned into syrup, which is turned into crystals. Simple enough, right?

High-fructose corn syrup, meanwhile, comes from—you guessed it—corn. For this type of refined sugar, the corn is milled in what we know as cornstarch, which then has a boatload of enzymes added to it. These enzymes increase the sugar content, making the corn syrup. The syrup is added to a bunch of things, like ice cream or jam, either to add flavor or bulk.

What may be surprising to some of you is that refined sugar, in all its forms, comes from natural sources. So, what about this type of sugar is so bad for you?

The key thing missing from refined sugar is fiber. This indigestible matter, which is found in abundance in fruits, for example, is essential for keeping your blood glucose from spiking beyond what is normal after a meal. Without fiber to help control your blood sugar, and therefore your insulin response, you get the full hit of sugar, which causes blood sugar problems, which, in turn, then causes health problems.

A diet high in fiber is super good for you in a lot of different ways, in fact, which is part of the reason keto is not all it's cracked up to be. Eating fruit is insanely healthy, and a perfectly reasonable source of natural sugars.

Okay, I think that clears that up. At least to the extent that we require it to be for the time being. So, let's move on to talking about what sorts of health problems we can run into when we allow our refined sugar consumption to get out of hand.

All the Ways Sugar Hurts Us

Okay, maybe not "all" the ways. That might be an enormous list, considering how bad this stuff is for us. But we should run over the big ones anyway, just so we get an idea of what we are dealing with.

Sugary beverages—sodas, in particular—are one of the main sources of refined sugar for most people. And if we drink too much soda, we wind up super unhealthy. For example, we will likely wind up with excess belly fat, which is generally considered to be the most dangerous form of fat (Schaefer & Yasin, 2023). It is, we are told, the type of fat most associated with heart disease and diabetes.

Another thing is that refined sugar interferes with a hormone called leptin, whose job it is to tell us when we are through eating. This might help to explain why some people seem able to hammer back a gazillion sugary candies in one sitting or drink a six-pack of colas.

And that, of course, is not all. Refined sugar has been linked to liver disease, which is no cakewalk. But maybe what is most interesting is that refined sugar has been linked to cognitive and emotional problems, like depression and dementia.

Let's just, for a second, focus on sugar's relationship to depression. Depression itself is a tricky illness, which is the result of a number of causes, many of which are still unknown to us. In fact, by just looking at the history of understanding depression, you will see that the nature of the illness, and particularly its causes, has remained elusive even into the modern period.

That said, there does appear to be some indication that refined sugar is linked to depression in middle age (Holland, 2020). This ultimately means that people who indulged excessively in refined sugars were more likely to develop depression as they entered middle age.

And what's more, the opposite is also true. People who ate whole foods were less likely to be diagnosed not just with depression, but with mood disorders generally.

How this happens is not 100% clear, however. One of the leading theories is that refined sugars are linked to inflammation, and inflammation is linked to depression. (I even once heard it said that depression might be best understood as an inflammatory disease. But since that is speculative and unproven, we should just flag it as interesting—if you think it is—and move on.)

Since men and women have different bodies, sugar affects us differently too. In fact, men appear to be at a greater risk of sugar's nasty side effects, including mood disorders. Among other things, this is definitely worth thinking about!

But remember, as we covered earlier, that it's not the quantity of sugars in general that affects us, but rather, it mostly comes down to the *types* of sugar we are ingesting. Sugars of the refined type are the ones that hurt us, while sugars in their natural state, i.e., in whole foods, are not only super good for us, but necessary for our survival.

So, not to belabor the point, but strawberries are not going to cause you to develop depression. Neither are whole grain pastas, bananas, carrots—none of that stuff. All of that should be included in your diet, barring some kind of medical reason.

And this is not to say that drinking a gazillion sodas a day is for sure going to make you depressed either. What it does, though, is increase the odds of you developing a mood disorder, including depression. This is probably done via inflammation, but really who knows? There might be some other cause we simply haven't identified yet.

In other words, taking in refined sugars comes with mental health risks, in addition to physical health ones. It's not just your body that suffers, but your ability to exist and interact in your environment is hindered—such is the case with mood disorders.

***

Okay, so I think I have made my point. Refined sugars are not only addictive, they are insanely bad for you.

The next question we will want to ask, then, is what exactly an addiction to sugar *looks* like. Furthermore, what are some of the warning signs? What are the symptoms of a sugar addiction, and what can we do to better our relationship with this granulated monkey on our backs?

Let's keep going and find out.

Chapter 2:

Identifying Sugar Addiction

A little personal information before we start this next chapter: I am, by all accounts, a hypochondriac. I get a tickle in my throat and I am convinced I have a terrible flu. A muscle cramp and I am sure that I have cancer. A little trouble remembering something and it is without a doubt the first sign of early dementia.

If you are anything like me, then you are reading about sugar addiction and worrying like crazy that you have one yourself. After all, do you not sometimes find yourself eating gummies while watching the Lifetime network and suddenly discover that all of the gummies are gone? What else could explain this level of compulsive behavior than an addiction that has gone unnoticed for quite some time?

Well, hopefully then by the end of this chapter, even the hypochondriacs among us will have been given some clarity. Because, as it turns out, there are real symptoms of being a sugar addict. And if you do not check any of these boxes, then it is safe to assume that this chapter does not apply to you. In which case, I am glad that I put that hypochondria to rest. (Although I know that's not how that works.)

However, there will be some of us to whom this applies maybe even too well. As such, this chapter will be doing double duty: Both easing our worries about whether or not we have a problem with sugar, and informing us—if we show these symptoms—that it might be time to think about making an intervention.

So, let's not dillydally any longer and get to investigating what exactly a sugar addiction looks like.

Signs and Symptoms

Getting right into it then, there are several clear signs that you have a sugar addiction. Some of them are more severe than others, while some of them are just downright annoying. Then, there are those that are just dangerous.

In other words, they run the whole gamut. But maybe the most obvious of these is the one that clearly indicates an addiction to anything, and that is the presence of withdrawal symptoms.

Now, what are withdrawal symptoms? Let's say you have an addiction to cigarettes—maybe not as common now as it once was, but an addiction we will all be familiar with at least conceptually nonetheless. The addictive chemical in cigarettes is called nicotine. It gives you a certain buzz when you smoke, generally understood to be stimulant-like, in that it speeds up your heart rate and increases your blood pressure.

This buzz activates your dopamine network. Your brain registers that it enjoys the feeling nicotine gives it, to where it makes a note to pursue this activity, and then, if this is done enough times, a habit is formed around smoking.

Your brain, in other words, becomes used to the presence of nicotine and depends upon its presence to stimulate certain neural networks, particularly dopamine. Once enough time passes, your nicotine levels drop, and your brain takes note of this. All the systems that have depended upon nicotine for their performance start to go squirrelly, which causes a whole host of bad feelings to appear. These bad feelings continue until your brain can sort itself out and learn to perform these functions without nicotine to stimulate them.

Such is withdrawal, generally speaking. Some drugs cause more severe withdrawal symptoms, particularly alcohol—its effects are so pernicious that quitting an alcohol habit should be done under a doctor's supervision. In fact, kicking a booze habit can lead to hallucinations, seizures, and even death.

Sugar, thankfully, is not as severe as alcohol. But if you have a sugar addiction, trying to quit or cut back will almost certainly lead to withdrawal symptoms.

What are these? Well, for starters, since dopamine gives you energy and a pleasurable feeling, if your dopamine network is dependent upon sugar in any capacity, these two feelings will turn into lethargy and crankiness.

Not only that, but since your blood sugar will drop dramatically, you will probably have headaches, muscle cramps, and nausea. And on top of *that*, you will likely experience insomnia, probably get the shakes, certainly have violent cravings, and maybe even enter a period of depression.

Still not as bad as alcohol, but also pretty severe, right? Those cravings, too, are another sign that a sugar addiction is present. After all, people normally do not have intense, almost uncontrollable urges to ingest something to which they are not addicted. But since, if you are withdrawing from sugar, your blood sugar will drop, your body will obviously notice this and send a signal that you should be eating more sugar in order to make up for this.

Basically, you wind up in a cycle of constantly chasing your insulin levels, which appears in your brain as a craving for sugar. Not exactly a walk in the park, to be blunt.

One of the weird symptoms of sugar addiction, however—and this is something I only learned in researching this book, so it blew my mind—is that the addiction causes a craving not just for sugar, but for *salt*.

As I said, this is a strange one. But it does make quite a bit of sense. See, one of the major features of refined sugar is that it has basically no nutritional value. And since all of the things we should be eating are such because we need their nutrients, filling ourselves up with nonnutritive foods means skipping out on the nutrition we need to survive.

In other words, you need vitamin C, for example, but you don't get that from eating sour candies. So, if you choose sour candies over fruit, you wind up with a vitamin deficiency. And considering how our bodies work, that means we will start craving foods we know provide things we are sorely lacking.

The problem with craving salty foods, in particular, is that we get most of our salt from things that are not good for us. Pizza, for example, or canned foods. This means that when we are short on salt and crave something salty, we are likely to reach for something that is unhealthy, and which, as it turns out, causes similar spikes and crashes to sugar.

For some people too, excess salt can mean heart problems in the future. So, skimping out on salt in favor of refined sugar and making up for this deficit with these types of foods could be deadly in the long run.

If thinking about problems with our organs is not enough to make you think twice about sugar addiction, there is always the fact that a sugar addiction is actually super bad for your skin to boot. And I'm not just talking about giving you acne, either.

As it turns out, sugar can actually cause your skin to *age* much faster than usual. Basically, how this works is the sugar weakens the proteins in your skin, which causes your skin to lose its firmness. In layman's terms, it sags.

And we're not done! A sugar addiction can lead to dry skin and wrinkles well before old age, which is when we normally expect to suffer those afflictions.

And also—yes—it causes acne. For skin health, this habit is basically as bad as it can get.

Additionally, that constant blood sugar spike-and-drop routine really does take a toll on your wakefulness. People will find themselves dozing off midday, in part because of that rise-and-fall pattern, but also because sugar interferes with an enzyme that, funny enough, helps to keep you awake during the day.

So, even using sugar as a stimulant is counterproductive. It makes you tired. This is sort of like when smokers say that they smoke because it relaxes them. It just doesn't make any sense. Nicotine increases your blood pressure. Any amount of relaxation you feel is either in your head, or you are misinterpreting the pleasurable sensation you got from dopamine.

But I digress.

Lastly, regarding your eating habits themselves: A sugar addict will, of course, find themselves eating when they are not hungry, because in this case, the purpose of eating is not satiation, but maintaining the dopamine high and staving off the withdrawal. But, in a move similar to one made by substance abusers, sugar addicts will often become self-conscious about their habit, and hide sugary snacks in order to keep their habit in the shadows.

Now, if this is you, I would say two things. First, you definitely have a problem. Keeping people in the dark about a sugar habit is a sure sign that things have gone off the rails and it is time for a course correction.

But also, to me, this means that you already know this is a bad habit. Right? You recognize on some level that what you are doing is harmful, or shameful, to the point where you are trying to keep it a secret.

Does this not mean you are already partway there? By "there" I mean, of course, taking the step to remove yourself from the problem and improve your life. Even if the conscious part of you is in denial, or is justifying your behavior in some way ("I'm not doing anything wrong, my friends are just judgmental"), some part of you disagrees with all this. Some part of you knows that this is unsustainable, or unhealthy, and should try and fix the problem.

What I am saying is, this seems like an awfully dark behavior, right? But there is a positive side to it—which is not nothing!

Anyway, so much for the symptoms of sugar addiction. The next question is, if we are worried about a sugar addiction, how do we go about getting diagnosed? Is there someone we can talk to, or some criteria we have to meet?

Diagnosing the Malady

Alright. We are getting into some tricky waters here. Things might get a little technical, but I am sure you can handle it. In the meantime, I will try to keep this as simple as possible.

"Sugar addiction" technically falls under the umbrella of "food addiction," which is itself a complicated topic. How, after all, is it possible to get addicted to something you need to consume in order to survive?

Well, a food addiction is in some sense an eating disorder; but in another sense, it shares a whole bunch of pathologies with substance use disorders. It also has a lot in common with "behavioral addictions" as well, such as compulsive gambling or porn addiction.

Why is this? Again, this comes down to the actual sugar itself. We do actually need sugar to survive, which means that it serves a nutritive function. But refined sugar also has a hedonic value, in that it makes us feel pleasure (Westwater et al., 2016).

Look at it like this: Cocaine has no nutritional value, but it has enormous hedonic value. This is what makes cocaine addiction a substance abuse disorder. Food, meanwhile, primarily has nutritional value and not much in the way of a hedonic value; maybe a little, but not in the same sense that cocaine or alcohol does. And yet, sugar itself is a substance that in some forms is refined (in a process not dissimilar to how cocaine is extracted), and which gives us a pleasurable feeling.

Now, a gambling addiction works in near-identical ways to a drug addiction, except that there is no substance involved; there is only the behavior—gambling. Eating is a lot like this, in that we can theoretically get the same pleasure value from all sorts of different foods, but the eating itself gives us pleasure. Hence, food addiction is a kind of behavioral addiction.

Food addiction is also literally an eating disorder, since it involves, tautologically, disordered eating. And since sugar is consumed by eating, then technically speaking, a sugar addiction would be an eating disorder.

So, what the heck is it, exactly?

The fact is that the jury is still out on this one. Any cursory glance at the literature will confirm too, that there is, at the very least, controversy around how to classify problematic sugar consumption.

This means, then, that diagnosing it is kind of an issue, right? What exactly can we say that a person is afflicted with when they are locked into this behavioral pattern? What are the solutions to it, i.e., the *treatment*? Is it treated like a behavioral or a substance addiction?

Well, in part, that is the focus of this very book. Because, since it exists in such a gray area, there are no rehabs one can go to. There are no AA-type meetings (that I'm aware of), and there are no methadone clinics.

Treatment, then, is a matter of self-control. Because, yes, this is not a classical addiction. It shares many properties with classical addictions, and refined sugar as a substance does bear many similarities to other addictive substances. However, it's just too ambiguous for us to understand at the moment, and so its status as a medical problem is more or less up for grabs.

Now, this is not to say that things like cognitive-behavioral therapy would not work. In fact, the success of those kinds of therapies has more than proven their effectiveness in treating all manner of ailments. And honestly, if you do have a sugar addiction, then this is a route you should absolutely consider. Involving a professional is always a good idea.

But even implementing that type of therapy comes down to hard work and self-control. It even, really, comes down to having a serious level of self-awareness.

With that in mind, how might we go about…

Understanding Our Relationship to Sugar

What a challenge!

I mean, for real. Even before we decide to see a therapist, there is always the question of whether or not a therapist is really necessary. And answering that question comes down to cultivating a self-awareness that is above and beyond what most people manage to pull off ever.

And it is not for nothing that we have such a hard time with this. Our minds are constructed in large part out of defense mechanisms. We deflect criticism from others super well, and from ourselves, we seem capable of pushing even the mildest criticism down into the depths. In fact, being self-critical is such a rare phenomenon that it is often seen as pathological before it even gets to the point of affecting our mental well-being.

And yet, this is exactly what we have to do with regard to our sugar habits.

Okay, where to start... Let's say we are watching TV, and we get an urge to eat a sugary snack. Maybe we have a craving for sour watermelons or something, just as an example. If we are worried that we might have a problematic relationship with sugar, we need to ask ourselves a really, really important question: *Why is it that I want to eat this right now?*

This is no idle question, as I am sure you know by now. Because the answer has a lot riding on it. What if the reason we want to eat the snack is because we have a habit of eating sugary nonsense and it has been so long since we have had such nonsense that our mood is starting to dip, and we need to re-up to keep ourselves from feeling sad?

What if we just had a hard day though, and this is simply a quick source of pleasure to help lift our spirits?

How do we know the difference?

There are a few ways, thankfully. The big thing I think is that it comes down to how much sugar we actually consume during a given day. If we go through several packs of sour watermelons every day, then odds are that our desire to have more is tainted in some capacity by our dopamine response. But what if we tend to just have one small bag at the end of the night once all our work is done, say, as a treat for having gotten through the grind?

You see the difference. The other thing, too, is that our mood is really an indicator of where we are at with sugar. You might ask yourself, "What will happen to my mood if I do not eat sugar? Will I just be disappointed? Or will I be full-blown depressed?"

I remember seeing an interview one time with the great wrestler Ric Flair. Many of you will know him as the guy who popularized saying "Wooo!" If anyone enjoys wrestling, they will know him as one of the great talents and performers in that industry. But if anyone is a fan of the man himself, they will know that he has had an enormous problem with alcohol throughout the entirety of his life.

In one interview, he was asked if he was an alcoholic. And the response he gave was interesting for several reasons. What he said was, "I don't know. I've never tried to quit."

Now, on the surface, this is kind of a funny thing to say. And it speaks to how defiant and wild the man is, as well as how much he seems to enjoy this lifestyle of being a party animal. But there is also a grain of truth to this—after all, if you never know how you react to being apart from a substance or habit, how would you know if you really are addicted to it?

Okay, obviously, there are ways you can determine this. With Flair, the fact that he, every day, drinks something like 15 double vodkas would indicate to most people that he has a problem. He has also had a number of medical procedures done on him as a result of his drinking, and one look at the quality of his skin shows that there is something else making him look like that beyond his old age.

But still—he's never been away from alcohol for long enough to know how much it affects him. And on some level, getting an answer to that question is really the most important one in terms of defining one's relationship to, say, alcohol. It's the thing that clears up all the ambiguities.

With sugar then, there really is a simple way to understand how it affects you: Try stopping. Remove sugar from your life for a week and see what happens.

If you find that you go through the gamut we have described here, from cravings all the way to withdrawal symptoms, then I think it is safe to assume you have a sugar addiction. And at this point, it is more than likely time to start rethinking our relationship with it and what you might try to do to get healthy again.

***

Okay, so much for the addiction itself. By now, though, I think we have a good idea not just of what that looks like in terms of its effects on our mental and physical health, but the limited treatment options at our disposal and how to figure out if we might be in the throes of this self-destructive behavior ourselves.

The next thing we will want to get into is learning how our internal and external factors affect our cravings for sugar. These are known as "triggers," and come in all shapes and sizes. Understanding them is one of the keys to understanding what makes us continue this behavior despite its obvious consequences.

So now, it's on to…

Chapter 3:

What Triggers Sugar Cravings

Addictions, whether we're talking about the substance or behavioral type, do not come from nowhere. In fact, people with addictions most often are using them to help deal with some type of trauma, either in the far past or more recently. Whenever it was, something *did* happen, and it is that thing onto which the addiction latches itself.

Not that this takes away from personal agency, of course. There is obviously an element of choice in the matter, in that a person with an addiction makes a conscious choice to at least begin using drugs. But the addiction seems to need trauma as a hook for it to take. And it is because of this that the compulsion to continue the addictive pattern often begins with what are called "triggers."

Now, let's just take a pause here: I know as well as anyone that this word has taken on a different meaning in the public space. And if you are anything like me, then the mention of this word will make your stomach seize up with the memories of people screaming at each other over one of them feeling "triggered." (Ironically, then, the word has become a kind of trigger in itself.)

But when I use this word, I am not using it in that sense. I mean it in a very real, clinical sense, in which a certain event, whether emotional, environmental, or of another type, leads to a desire to do whatever it is that the subject is addicted to. These are the things that dig into our brains, make us feel something we would rather not feel, and lead us to continuing the self-destructive behavior we have been partaking in.

There are a whole bunch of different types of these. And needless to say, we do not have enough time to go through every possible one. But we will try to get a good sense of what these triggers might be and why they contribute to the addiction cycle.

This means for us, specifically, that we are interested in what sorts of things might happen which lead a person to make an immediate choice to consume refined sugar.

To start us off then, we will talk about…

Emotional Triggers

For me, these are maybe the most obvious ones when we talk about what would cause someone to have an immediate desire to consume, in this case, refined sugar, if and when they are addicted to it. After all, a negative emotional state can theoretically be solved in the short term by substance use, right? Sugar gives us a dopamine high, dopamine is the pleasure chemical, pleasure is the opposite of "feeling bad," and presto—the bad feeling gets turned into a good feeling!

Which types of emotions might we be talking about, though? There are a whole bunch, but let's go through some of the more common ones.

Maybe the most obvious one is depression. This disease is characterized by a whole slew of the least-desirable feelings possible, and, as such, it causes an unreal amount of suffering in people who go through it. Basically, your ability to feel good feelings is annihilated, and your ability to feel bad things is cranked up to unbearable levels. And this state can last for weeks at a time, or even longer.

As you can see, depression is much more than just sadness. It is a state that is utterly debilitating. Everything feels cold and lifeless. All meaning is stripped away. Hope ceases to be. And there seems to be no point in doing absolutely anything—provided you could even get the energy to do something in the first place.

Now, this is another thing about depression: You actually wind up doing things more slowly. Even talking! If you ever talk to someone who is depressed, you will notice that words come out of them like molasses. This applies to walking, too, or even getting off the couch. (Which is why, incidentally, the common advice that someone in the throes of depression "get some exercise" is about as worthless a piece of advice as you can imagine.)

When someone is in this state, there are a few options regarding how they can feel toward it. But most commonly, in my experience, there is either a resigned feeling, in the sense that they feel they must deserve this feeling, or that there would be simply no sense in alleviating it; or, that they desperately want to *not* feel like that, and will do almost anything to make the symptoms go away.

It is this second way of feeling that can be either positive or negative. (The first is just a total bummer.) It can be positive because it can motivate people to get help. But conversely, it can be negative in that it can drive people to drink, take drugs, or engage in all manner of unhealthy and dangerous behaviors.

For sugar then, the connection is clear. Since sugary foods make us feel pleasure, this sense of pleasure can theoretically alleviate the depression. For some people, it might even work quite well. And if not, it might be super good at masking the problem.

Here, we might also implicate depression's close cousin, anxiety. This is another misunderstood illness, in that it is much more than just feeling worried. It is an overpowering sense of fear, which can cause sufferers to skip out on huge chunks of their lives, just to avoid feeling the sheer terror that comes with doing whatever it is that causes them anxiety.

General anxiety is a condition that goes above and beyond even worrying about a specific thing. See, while social anxiety is being pathologically worried about social situations, and phobias refer to pathologic anxieties about specific fear objects (spiders, heights), general anxiety means being constantly worried about virtually everything.

Can an addiction use anxiety as its hook to latch onto you as well? Absolutely. Plenty of people use addiction to cope with their anxiety, from people who need to have a few drinks before being social, to people who use the pleasure they get from eating doughnuts and cookies to calm that constant chatter of worry.

Now, the reason I started off with depression and anxiety is that most other emotional triggers are related to these two in some way. Consider, for example, feeling isolated and lonely. What sorts of feelings does this conjure? Sure, feeling lonely is an emotion in itself. But it implies sadness also, does it not?

What about people who get saddled with a big workload and feel overwhelmed? That can cause someone to indulge in their vice too, of course. But does being overwhelmed not imply a kind of anxiety?

Worry and sadness, in other words, tend to be the species of emotional trigger, while all others fall into one or the other as a genus. Or, to put it more simply, loneliness is a subcategory of sadness as much as being overwhelmed is a subcategory of worry.

With these two categories in mind, we can work out what all the other emotional triggers might be. Mourning the loss of a loved one, starting a new job, getting a divorce, someone insulting you, anticipating a difficult conversation—the list goes on.

Any and all of these things can start the thought process which leads to a decision to indulge in your sugar habit, just as much as it leads someone to gamble or drink. So, if sugar addiction is an issue for you, it would be in your best interest to figure out which of these emotional states is most likely to lead you to indulge, and then find a strategy to deal with that.

But, of course, emotional triggers aren't the only kind. There are also…

Environmental Triggers

Where we are and what we are around is a huge part of what eases us along the path of problematic sugar use. This is interesting because in these scenarios, it is not that we are masking our emotions with sugar eating, but that we are made to experience memories of what consuming sugar is like; and it is this that sets us on the path to doing so again.

What do I mean by this? Well, Christmas is a time of year when most Westerners indulge in poor eating habits. On the sugary side of things, this means eating candy canes and cookies and drinking eggnog.

Christmas is also notable because there are all kinds of visual cues to remind us of what time it is. Red and green lights, tinsel… For those of us in the north, there is also snow, which is intimately connected to memories of Christmas. And, of course, many of us visit our families, often spending at least some time at our parents' homes.

Walking into our mom and dad's house, say, while it is snowing outside, to find the place covered in tinsel and mistletoe, as well as to find that our dad is wearing a Santa hat and our mom is wearing a baking apron—this scenario comes loaded with sense memories. And one of those will certainly be food, be it the taste or smell, and the memories of consuming that food.

We see then how this works in other areas too. We follow a friend into a bakery or go into a restaurant where we used to eat mounds of ice cream. The location itself is tied to memories of sugar eating, and once those memories arise, they inevitably lead to the thought that we should indulge in that habit which made us feel so good the last several times we did it.

And it is not just a location that can do this to us, either. Being around people who are indulging in our vice is also an environmental trigger. Again, this is because it causes us to remember our own previous indulgences. We see someone eating a cookie, or snacking on sour candies, and it makes us remember our own experiences. Remembering that experience causes our brain to suggest we come up with a plan to reenact that experience, and if we are not careful, this will lead to us reenacting that plan in real life.

Anyone and everyone with a vice has environmental triggers. And they are just as important to identify as emotional ones.

And by the way, while we're on this topic, let me mention that I'm currently writing this as Christmas approaches, so writing specifically about Christmastime as a host for environmental triggers has gotten me thinking. Is there a time of year that is more likely to make people want to indulge in their vices?

I mean, the idea that Christmas is stressful really gets thrown around a lot, but I don't think it gets the credit it is due. For being a holiday that is all about cheeriness and togetherness, it is remarkably stressful. And not just because for people north of the equator it happens during the darkest period of the year, either. It is just an utter smorgasbord of troublesome, grating experiences, which naturally lends itself to making the decision to *use* again.

Okay, I know, I know. That's an awfully negative thing to say. And I agree! So, let me dial this in a bit. I understand that there are plenty of things to love about Christmas. I also understand the importance of having a time of year when we dedicate ourselves to showing love and appreciation for one another.

But also, is the relentless optimism not a bit on the trying side? I refuse to believe I am the only one who feels this way. I mean, I am only a human being, after all. I experience a whole slew of emotions. Some of them are quite negative, in fact. Having to be positive for a whole holiday season can sometimes feel like hard work!

Alright, I am being a bit of a grinch. But look, this is the only thing about the holidays that bothers me, right? Everybody, I am convinced, has at least *one thing* about the holidays that bothers them. Even my dad, who is the most Clark Griswold dad who ever lived, and who starts listening to Christmas songs in October, gets stressed and sad over the holidays. Why? Because the holidays cannot possibly match the completely unrealistic level of hype he builds up in his own imagination.

Moving on, maybe we have to see family members we do not get along with. Maybe we know we are going to get asked questions about our personal lives we have no interest in answering. Maybe last Christmas we brought home a romantic partner who is not coming this year for reasons we would rather not discuss, but we know grandma is going to be really persistent about asking.

What I'm saying is, these are known as stressful times for a reason. And if we are working on changing a problematic habit of ours, whether sugar or otherwise, Christmas is basically an open minefield of opportunities to blow our progress.

This is no more true than, I would argue, for both sugar and alcohol. Those are the two things that tend to be indulged in the most during this period—at least in my experience. What this means is that you will need to be prepared, and have some kind of a plan, because the end of the year is going to be a trying time.

Luckily for you, we are going to talk about some strategies later in the book. But for now, we should simply flag Christmas as a time when there are bound to be some significant challenges.

Alright, enough of this. We know about emotional and environmental triggers. But what about...

Psychological Triggers

Now, you might be thinking, "Isn't this kinda the same as emotional triggers?" And you are partly right, in a way. Emotional triggers are certainly a *kind* of psychological trigger, in a literal sense. But here, "psychological" has a slightly different meaning.

See, we human beings act on our beliefs. If we believe, say, that people should be treated with respect, then we treat people with respect. If we believe that petty arguments at the bar are best solved with fisticuffs, well, we tend to settle petty, drunken arguments with physical violence.

Let's say, then, that we believe hopefulness is a kind of delusion. Maybe we believe that being "realistic" means thinking that any and all attempts at change will inevitably end in failure, and so trying to change anything for the better is an utter waste of time. The best we can do, in fact, is accept how awful everything is and learn to tolerate this until we die.

I know, a bit melodramatic. Nonetheless, this is an opinion many people have, especially people with addictions.

Now, give this person a sugar habit. Even a hefty one, that has come with physical consequences, all of them undesirable. Explain to them that if they continue to indulge in this habit, these problems will only worsen, until, perhaps, they die. How are they going to view this information?

Even if they temporarily acquiesce to whatever you have told them, maybe out of mortal terror, if they truly believe that all attempts at change will end in failure, then that thought will arise again. And when it does, it will trigger the thought that, therefore, they should just enjoy their habit, regardless of the consequences.

Or maybe this is too specific a belief system for you. Fair enough. Let's look at a simpler one. What if someone sincerely believes that they are not worth fixing? Maybe they think that it's fine and good for other people to change their ways, but they are not worth concerning even themselves over.

In other words, this someone is genuinely self-hating. It is a common side effect of depression, certainly. They can accept that this or that habit will lead to poor health outcomes, and that, in most cases, cutting out the habit leads to the good. They can accept that, therefore, if they were to stop their sugar addiction, they would become healthier.

The question is: "Why should I want to be healthier? I'm not worth anything. Being unhealthy is what I deserve."

Obviously, this thought process also triggers the desire to eat sugar. And if the desire to eat sugar is not tempered by a desire to become healthy, then the desire to eat sugar will become *the action of eating sugar.*

So, yes, what we believe affects whether or not we make healthy choices. And if a sugar habit is already a symptom of depression? Well, you can see how depressive thought patterns are self-reinforcing. It's a genuinely difficult cycle to get out of!

Another thing depression can lead to is something called rumination. This is a thought pattern in which you focus excessively on something negative, and for long periods of time. For example, you might keep remembering something embarrassing that happened when you were a kid, or you might not be able to stop thinking about something mean someone said to you once, maybe even a long time ago. And it doesn't have to be a memory either. It can be anything negative, like how you are not good enough, or nobody likes you, or something like that. But what happens is, you start thinking about that negative thing, and then you have a terrible time getting out of it. You keep thinking those negative thoughts over and over again.

This cycle can, of course, trigger a desire to eat sugar. Rumination, as I can attest to from experience, is a horrific state to be in. And as I said, getting out of it can be quite the challenge. If you have already trained your brain to use sugar as a means of getting away from rumination, then you can imagine how hard it can be to pry yourself away from a box of doughnuts.

Another psychological state that is likely to lead to sugar consumption is a state of unfair judgment about oneself. Now, as a caveat, a state of perfectly fair judgment of oneself might also lead to sugar consumption, if you are fairly judging yourself as being guilty of something you are absolutely guilty of. But an unfair judgment of oneself is, I have found, far more common than the latter. If only because, so far as I can tell, human beings are not, on the whole, super good judges of, frankly, anything.

But in this state, you maintain a belief that you are guilty of something to a greater degree than you are in reality. (Again, belief is the key issue with these triggers.) Human beings are endowed with a sense of justice, which, in part, is necessarily retributive. We believe, generally, that people who have committed a crime, or a sin, or who are guilty of a moral transgression, owe something in response for what they have done.

This might sound barbaric to some, but it really is the core of our concept of justice. A fine is maybe the most civilized example. When someone commits a crime, they are deprived of a certain amount of their earnings, in recompense for what they have done.

This goes for literally everything else in justice. If someone commits an act of violence, they have to enter a period in which their rights are suspended, such that they "owe" their freedom to society. This is deemed fair, because someone who has committed a crime has, in a sense, misused their freedom. Or, to put it better, they have interfered with the freedom of another person, and so owe their freedom in response.

Obviously, I am not trying to give a lesson in legal theory here. The point I am making is that we intuitively understand justice as requiring someone to give up something of theirs in return for their transgression.

So, what happens if we hold ourselves accountable for something we have done? What if we believe wholeheartedly that we have done something horrific to someone else, even when that belief does not correspond to reality?

Consider the following: Some people whose loved ones have died say they feel a sense of relief following this event. This is, most of the time, because their loved one was suffering for a long period, and their death is seen as a kind of reprieve, or rest from their suffering. The sense of relief stems from the fact that the period of trial has ended.

And yet, this relief can be catastrophic to some people. They report all manner of guilty feelings, even so far as experiencing a sense of revulsion toward themselves. "What kind of evil person am I," they ask, "who can be happy that my beloved husband is dead?"

We know objectively that anyone holding themselves accountable for this thought is being too hard on themselves. And yet, that is what happens with some people. They see themselves as being guilty, of having done something unthinkable.

What do they "owe" for having transgressed?

Again, objectively, they owe nothing at all. But the subjective sense that one is guilty, followed by the incessant judging of oneself for being guilty, inevitably summons this thought. Justice is intuitive, remember.

Well, for many people, this means entering a period of self-punishment. Maybe one of drinking excessively, or smoking. Not exercising. These are types of self-mortification, like Medieval Catholics whipping themselves.

And so, not to sound like a broken record, but if you throw a sugar habit in the mix…?

Of course, the worst part about this scenario is that no amount of showing how bad sugar is for someone is going to persuade them to cut it out. How unhealthy it is *is the whole point.* This person is taking their own pound of flesh via the unhealthy consumption of something that is bad for them.

Alright, I think I have made my point. Psychological triggers are beliefs but also thought patterns in general, which promote the idea that one should indulge in the habit of consuming sugar.

Recognizing which thought patterns do this to you, if any, is a key step in getting ahead of them. Forewarned is forearmed, as they say.

***

I think this chapter has given a decent rundown of what sorts of triggers might lead to a desire to consume sugar. There are others too, and if you are perceptive and make an effort to do so, you will be able to notice your own and make a plan so as to not have them affect you.

Temptation, as they say, is always with us. But being vigilant is a choice.

But now that we know where some of our desire to eat sugar might come from, I think we need to get onto which sorts of tactics we might use to combat them. Vigilance is all fine and good, but knowing how to beat the temptations is where the money's really at.

So, that said, it's time to get into discussing some of these techniques to help fight sugar addiction head-on.

Chapter 4:

Methods to Break Free From

Sugar Addiction

Alright, where were we?

So far, we have covered what sugar addiction is, which types of sugar we become addicted to, how to identify if we have the condition, and what sorts of triggers there might be that would cause us to want to use the stuff.

In other words, we have laid a decent groundwork for getting into the real details of the topic. Because here, we want to dig into what to do, in a practical sense, to fight against this scourge of a thing.

Now, as we go through this, I should mention that this is not exactly foolproof. Every person reacts differently to different things, and with these suggestions, there will be some that work for some people and some that do absolutely nothing whatsoever. This is why they are *suggestions*—things to get you started and experimenting until you find the one that works best for you.

What's more, these are things you can do yourself, which means this does not cover talking to doctors or therapists, which, under certain circumstances, is 100% advised. (In fact, if you are this far into a sugar habit that you need strategies to help combat it, talking to a doctor would be a good idea anyway.)

With that in mind, what sorts of things can we do ourselves, at home, to fight against the sugar addiction?

Dieting

This is a simple one. So simple, in fact, that it may sound stupid.

But its simplicity is its greatest asset. See, if you have a sugar addiction, you will experience cravings for the refined sugar that has become a daily habit for you. This, of course, we have discussed already. What it means, though, is that you have a desire either to eat or drink something which means that eating or drinking something else could possibly help curb the craving altogether.

Okay, fine. But what kind of food or drink should we use?

That's the easiest part. Sugar, as we know, exists in the world naturally. Just about everything we eat and drink has sugar in it, in fact, which means there are a whole host of things we can use to get *some* sugar, but in a healthier way.

Citrus fruits, for example, are a great replacement. An orange, when ripe, is wicked sweet—and unbelievably good for you. But if they are not your thing, then there are obviously lots of fruits out there that can do the job, from bananas to apples, and even more exotic ones like dragon fruit.

Now, if you object to eating fruit, you might be in for some trouble. First off, fruit is an important part of any diet.

Secondly, you already have a sweet tooth. Why not enjoy nature's candy?

The other thing is that if your sugar addiction comes in the form of eating things—i.e., candy—then replacing it with something to eat is going to help. Consider smoking: When some people quit, they replace the addiction with eating Scotch Mints. This is because they get at least some of the sensations or rituals they had with smoking in a different form. They unwrap the package, take out the item pop it in their mouth... They even get a unique sensation when breathing, this time from the coolness of the mint.

If your sugar addiction is one from drinking, however, this is obviously different. And actually, I would argue, much more complicated.

Because, while you obviously want to replace it with something else to drink, the question remains: Just what the heck can replace drinking sodas?

A lot of people will tell you to replace it with water, which is sound advice in itself, but water is not sweet. And if you start using those sugary squirt bottles to put flavor into the water, then you haven't exactly solved your problem.

This is where sugar replacements can be your friend, but there are some caveats here. If you find that using something like stevia throws you for a loop and puts you into a craving spiral, then you will want to avoid it at all costs. This is a real risk too. Lots of people report this happening to them.

If this is you, then you will want to rethink your plan of attack. Maybe you need a combination of things, like fruit and water— one of these to satisfy the urge for sweetness, and one for the act of drinking something. But if, despite all your experimentation you come up with nothing, I strongly recommend you talk to your doctor.

If, however, you find that it does satisfy the craving? Then great! Use it. No notes, no caveats. If you run into problems, you can address them as they arise. But for now, you are trying to kick your sugar habit, and if this works, then this works.

Diet, then, in the form of food or liquid, is going to be our friend in getting past the cravings. Choosing which foods to replace our habit with might take experimentation and it might take some time. But it is one of the essential ways to help curb the need for refined sugar.

Alright, so much for diet. What else can we talk about? How about...

Lifestyle Changes

This is both more complicated and more demanding than the previous suggestion. Why? Because our lifestyle is pretty well-ingrained. We have habits that make up our routine, for example. We have ways that we prefer to relax, and we know how we like to spend our social time with one another.

Changing these, therefore, is unbelievably challenging. But, for altering self-destructive behavior, it is also absolutely essential.

But which lifestyle choices might be responsible for our sugar habit to begin with? Or, if not exactly "responsible for," which ones contribute to our ongoing sugar habit? And what can we do to alter those?

An easy one to start with is what is known as the "sedentary lifestyle." Now, this is a broad one. After this, we will deal with smaller, more specific lifestyle choices. But I wanted to start off with one that represents an overall approach to being in the world, to show how it might lead to compulsive sugar eating.

Someone who lives a sedentary lifestyle is, as the name suggests, not moving around a whole lot. This is someone who maybe works from a desk, but who does not exercise after work. This is someone who comes home, sits on the couch, turns on the TV, and stays there until it is time to lie down and sleep.

As you can imagine, this lifestyle is susceptible to all manner of poor habits. Setting aside even that this is incredibly bad for your body in itself, people who live a sedentary lifestyle do not have much to occupy themselves with, aside from whatever entertainment they have running. So, what else are they to do, say, with their hands?

Let me be more specific. Of the people in my life who are largely sedentary, every single one of them has a vice of some sort that they should consider doing away with. That includes at least one with an alcohol habit, a few who smoke, several who are enormous potheads... But more often than not, they tend to have poor eating habits.

I could go over to their house at any time while they are at home, and they will have a bag of chips open. Or they will be drinking sodas and watching YouTube videos of people falling off skateboards. Every one of these people has weight problems, and one of them is staring down the barrel of diabetes.

These two things—the sedentary lifestyle and poor diet choices—even down to problematic, or addictive diet choices, seem to go hand in hand. But how?

I'll tell you my theory: I think the thing both of these choices have in common is that they are really simple ways to obtain pleasure. When it comes to sitting down all the time, well, exercise is hard—no doubt. It takes effort. You *will* feel super good afterward. But it takes effort.

Lying on the couch and watching sports highlights gets our dopamine going, of course. But unlike exercise, to do so requires no effort. In fact, in order to accomplish this task, it is essential that you be totally passive.

So, too, is the case with diet choices. Sugar is, as we know, a really simple and quick way to get a dopamine high. Refined sugar is administered in large doses via small amounts of food or drink. And getting hold of it is super easy. You just buy it from the store, consume it, and feel good.

The solution to this lifestyle problem, then, is more complicated than the others we will talk about in a second. The solution here is an almost full-scale reworking of our attitude toward pleasure itself, and how we obtain it.

And yet, like any change in lifestyle, the key here is to start with small things and to do one thing at a time. If you try to change too much too quickly, you will almost certainly fail. So here, maybe, you want to start with the obvious: Is all that sitting around really good for you? Would it not be better to try exercising at least a couple of times a week?

The trick is to train your body and your mind to slowly accept that working for pleasure is much more rewarding than getting immediate hits of it. This is, again, the root problem that led to a sedentary lifestyle *and* a desire to consume refined sugar at such dangerous levels. Once you accomplish this level of rethinking, the problem of sugar consumption should be much easier to solve.

As I said, this one takes time, since it is a whole-picture, whole-system error. But there are other lifestyle choices that are not so all-encompassing, and which can be fixed much more easily.

For example, you might not have the best-organized day, which can lead to you being frustrated, which can then lead to you eating sugar. This fix is literally just for you to start organizing your day better. You will be less scattered, less frustrated, and less prone to eating sugar.

Maybe you have been keeping yourself up late and not getting enough sleep, which has made you feel moody, and has thus made you drink sugary drinks throughout the day. If that is the case, you need to consider reworking things so you can get the sleep you need, and thereby keep you away from those drinks.

The list goes on and on. But you see the pattern now, I hope. A system-wide lifestyle error is going to take much more work to fix but can be addressed through incremental changes. And smaller, more manageable ones can be tackled much more easily, even if they can be just as responsible for poor eating habits. Either way, you have the power and ability to fix these things if you so choose. And doing so will certainly help you!

Okay, what else can we talk about?

The Role of Exercise in Curbing Cravings

People who do not already exercise have a difficult time starting. I know, because there was a time when I did not exercise myself. The idea of starting, of running every day, or of lifting weights, seemed impossible. It seemed like work and pain, and I was not sure I was in the mood to add those two things into my life.

But guess what? Once you start exercising, you totally get the bug. It's fun, it's super good for you, and, as it turns out, it can totally help you with sugar cravings.

Part of this comes down to dopamine again. See, when you exercise, your brain releases a flood of dopamine, which tells you that this is a pleasurable activity, and also that it should be pursued again. Because of how dopamine affects your brain, this means converting the whole process of getting exercise into a memory, specifically a procedural memory, meaning you remember how to get a hold of this activity so that you can do it again.

What does this mean? Well, think of the whole process leading up to exercise. You put on your workout clothes, maybe. Fill up a water bottle. Put on your running shoes. Every one of these steps is part of the memory of how to begin exercising. And since your brain wants you to exercise, it releases dopamine at every step too. This, then, means even just tying your laces gives you a feeling of pleasure.

And that says nothing about the actual exercising itself, which results in a surge of dopamine that makes you feel insanely good. Basically, you wind up with a prolonged release of the stuff, making you feel good every step of the way.

Sugar addiction also works off the dopamine cycle. And part of the problem, as we know, when you try to kick the stuff, is that you wind up being low on dopamine. And when you are low on dopamine, you feel terrible.

What better way to curb this feeling than by doing something else which produces the same effect? Only this time, it is something that is healthy for you, does not age your skin prematurely, or runs the risk of giving you diabetes.

So, with regard to developing a plan to tackle even the strongest sugar cravings, exercise is going to do you wonders. Especially, I might add, if and when it is combined with diet. Which, in combination with adequate sleep, still remains the most surefire way to become the healthiest version of yourself possible.

But, of course, even with all that, there is still the persistent influence of stress in most of our lives. So, maybe we should talk about…

Stress Management Techniques

Yes, for most of us, stress is a perennial. It could be from our jobs, our families, or, more often than not, money. It is an unavoidable fact of life, from which, frankly, there is no escape.

Now, I do not mean to sound dire. Stress itself is obviously inevitable because nothing in life is ever always going to go according to plan. There is always conflict and strife; always expectations that go unmet. The question, really, is how we handle stress when it *does* arrive.

And this is much more important than we sometimes give it credit for. Stress has all kinds of negative impacts on our lives. It can lead to poor brain health, cancer, heart problems… A stressful life, in other words, can put us into an early grave.

But it is also an invitation to take up a vice. This is why people, say, drink after work. It is why people smoke cigarettes or spend every weekend at the casino. And it is for sure one of the reasons people turn toward sugary snacks and drinks as a means of helping to cope with the stress they feel.

So, what do we do if we feel stressed? How do we handle this wretched, all-consuming feeling?

There are several ways we can approach stress. But for me, the thing that has helped me the most is mindfulness practice.

A little backstory: I have spent a good chunk of my life in a state that I would call, "quite stressed out." Anxious, you might even say. It is very easy for me to slide into a state of fear, sometimes about something quite specific, sometimes about nothing at all. When left to my own devices, I am often in a state of mortal terror.

This used to cause me a whole host of problems. I would miss out on things, not get my work done… It even got in the way of a few relationships, if I am being frank. But at a certain point, it became obvious that I was not handling the stress very well, and so I decided to give tackling it head-on a try.

One of the things that stood out to me was mindfulness meditation. Now, I know "mindfulness" gets thrown around a lot. It is basically a useless term by now since it supposedly applies to everything from eating to shopping online.

But it really does mean something concrete, beyond being a kind of brand label. And what it means—what the action of "practicing mindfulness" is—is something that is very, very helpful.

Essentially, how it works is like this: You start off by, well, meditating. To do this, you sit in a comfortable position. Not necessarily the lotus position, which you see in movies, but a comfortable one. While you sit, you close your eyes, and you focus on your breath. When your attention drifts, you come back to your breath, without chastising yourself or judging yourself or anything else.

What you learn when you do this is that your thoughts come and go without you having any control over them. (Freudians would say they are arising from the unconscious.) They are, in a way, like waves, if you imagine that your mind is a kind of ocean. You can "watch" them even—how they show up and go away, arise and disappear. You can even, and this is crucial, distance yourself from them, becoming an observer of your thoughts without getting lost in them.

If you get more advanced, you can try this with your emotions. Here, you will find the same thing. You might think of something that makes you happy or angry. And when the emotion arises, you can notice, from a distance, how this emotion manifests physically *and* mentally. But, significantly, without being *consumed* by it.

For example, when I am angry, my shoulders tense. They come almost all the way up to my ears. I get a kind of burning feeling in my stomach and I clench my teeth. By approaching this mindfully, however, I can see that this emotion manifests, that I experience it, but I can simply notice it and let it go on its way. Just like any other thought.

This might sound a tad silly to you, but I promise it works! You can learn this skill, figure out how to use it more effectively, and then become better at conquering your emotions, instead of letting them conquer you.

What this means for stress and sugar addiction, is that when we become stressed, it is possible for us to not be consumed by it. Indeed, we can learn to observe our stress, even learn from it, without letting it sit in the pilot's seat.

If we can do that, then we are less likely to have stress lead us to eat refined sugar. We become the master of our stress and thereby become the master of our eating habits.

As I say, this works really well for me. Maybe it won't work for you, but I recommend giving it a whirl anyway. You never know—maybe this is exactly what you need to help manage those negative emotions.

***

Okay, I think I have made my point.

We know now that there are several methods by which we can tackle our cravings for sugar. We can use healthy food, begin an exercise regimen, make subtle or even large-scale lifestyle changes, and develop mindfulness practices. And we can do these things all with the intention of managing not just our cravings, but the reasons why we might be craving sugar in the first place.

This is all a part of becoming healthier, right? The more directions we can come at this problem from, the better. It is only going to help us.

And yet, I feel like there is more to say about diet, don't you? I feel like, since eating sugar is fundamentally about *eating something*, we should really dig deep to figure out what kind of food alternatives we can choose that will help replace our problematic sugar consumption.

It is time to take a deep dive into food, grocery shopping, and the healthy replacements we can use to satisfy the ol' sweet tooth.

Chapter 5:

Choosing Healthier

Alternatives

"Diet" is not a particularly nice word, is it? For most of us, we hear it as a verb, as when we say someone "is dieting," or if as a noun, it's usually referring to the activity in which we constrain our eating choices down to an unnatural level of self-denial.

And it is not for nothing, either, that we think of it in this way. Many of the diets people have gone on throughout history have been, quite frankly, insane. There are diets where people only eat grapefruits for a month or some ultra-extreme ones where people only eat tree bark.

We also know about yo-yo dieting, where someone adopts a diet that is successful, only to gain all the weight they lost back when they go off the diet. This process goes on *ad infinitum*. Hence, "yo-yo."

When I am talking about our diet though, I do not want it to come with these connotations. Not least because I am using "diet" in the most general sense, meaning "what we eat." But also, even though I am talking about alterations and substitutions and the like, I do not want this to sound as though I am advocating restriction and self-denial.

Instead, I would prefer that we think about this as something much closer to "substitution." Although we are in a literal sense talking about getting rid of refined sugars (or at least nearly doing so), we do not want to wind up in a place where there is no more room for the enjoyment of food. We want, instead, to replace the refined sugars with food that is both enjoyable *and* healthy.

There is no reason this process should be painful. In fact, if nothing else, it should be kind of fun. You get to make adjustments, try on a new lifestyle choice... Who doesn't like a fresh start?

And why don't we start, then, with some simple, low-sugar foods we can use to replace the high-sugar ones we have been eating so far?

Low-Sugar Replacement Foods

For those of us who consume high amounts of refined sugars, our palates might have a bit of a hard time with these foods. In fact, just looking at them might make us think there is no *way* we would eat any of this stuff.

And I hear you. Alas, resetting our palates is going to be an important step in getting off the refined sugars. And these foods, while maybe not the sweetest, are extremely good for us, and will help keep our healthiness up as we, possibly, enter into a period of restlessness and withdrawal.

Which foods am I talking about?

Firstly, vegetables. Now, I get that these foods might have a bad reputation among some people. They are often thought of as bland and boring. I actually used to have a neighbor, by the way, who bragged that he never ate vegetables. He ate meat, potatoes, and snacks, and his beverages of choice were usually whiskey and Coca-Cola. Incidentally, he also weighed over 500 pounds and died of a heart attack in his early 50s.

He was a good guy too. So, it was an awful shame.

But on top of being essential for your health, they really do taste good. You just maybe haven't gotten used to them yet. Or maybe, to start off with, you need to prepare them using spices.

Or maybe you just haven't found the right ones! Maybe you don't like carrots but you like cucumber. Maybe you don't like broccoli but you like cauliflower. There are more types of vegetables than you can possibly imagine, which means there are at least some out there that suit your palate.

Either way, if your feelings toward vegetables are negative, this is something you will need to work on. They are maybe the most essential part of every diet and should never be skimped on.

Additionally, whole grains are low sugar. What we're talking about here are brown rice, quinoa, and oats. This means for breakfast, you can make some oatmeal and throw in some fresh fruit. This is my go-to, anyway.

Another thing is that proteins do not contain sugar. This means seafood, soybeans—stuff like that—are all fair game. So, in terms of resetting your palate or finding your way around tastes other than sugar, this might be a good route to experiment with.

But remember that just because we are getting away from refined sugar does not mean we want to try the keto diet. We need sugars, we just need them in forms that do not cause us harm. So, the fact that fish does not have sugar might be, as I said, good for getting used to different flavor sensations, but for health reasons, not having sugar is totally neutral. You still need sugar, just as much as you need protein.

All in all, there are quite a few food arenas you can play around in to find flavors you enjoy. And if you stick to foods like vegetables, grains, and seafood, you really are doing your health a favor.

But, of course, we are here because, alas, we do have a sweet tooth. So, what sorts of sweet foods can we—*should* we—be eating to help replace our intake of candy and sodas?

How to Satisfy Your Sweet Tooth in a Good Way

The answer to this, of course, is *fruit*.

Let me tell you this: I *love* fruit. I could eat fruit all day. I like experimenting with it too, whether by trying out new ones or opting for ones from different parts of the world. I used to live next to a greengrocer and every day they would have new exotic fruits out. After living there for almost two years, there is a good chance I have tried most of the exotic fruits that have ever been brought into this fair country.

My favorite, though? Let me take a bit of a detour here. My favorite fruit is, without a doubt, blood orange.

Why, you ask? Well, to begin with, they look fantastic. There is something about them still being an orange that really attracts me. The fact that with each one, the red color runs through it a little more or a little less, makes them all unique. And how that affects the taste means that there is such a broad spectrum of blood orange flavors.

It's a fruit that is surprising, in other words. Aesthetically pleasing, flavorful, and surprising. What's not to like?

Maybe for you, though, the fruit you gravitate toward is something else. Maybe you like grapes or bananas, or one of the many different kinds of apples. Maybe you like pears, clementines, tangerines, watermelon. Maybe you like cantaloupe or honeydew.

Maybe you like the exotic ones like dragon fruit. Myself, I love mangoes. But I am also a huge fan of the papaya. Most people dismiss the papaya because it can be bitter, but when it's ripe, it has a wonderful creamy flavoring. And they are fun to prepare because they have what I can only guess are a billion seeds in them—seeds that look almost like wet coffee beans.

Anyway, my point is that there is a variety to fruit, which means it is an accommodating food arena. Fruits are, by their nature, sweet, which means they should be a useful substitute for the refined sugars we have developed a habit for. And no amount of fruit, as it turns out, is too much.

Beyond fruit, there are, of course, dairy products like yogurt, which are sweet and healthy. Certain low-fat cheeses might also be advisable and can even be found mixed with dried fruit, like blueberries.

My point here is that there is no reason why getting away from sugary snacks and beverages should mean having to forgo sweetness in our diet completely. In fact, we can even up the amount of sweet food we eat every day, so long as they are coming from healthy sources.

I am not kidding when I say you can just eat fruit all day. You can make it a huge part of every meal, you can make it your snack—whatever you want. When you get tired of fruit, you can go to yogurt or cheese. You can attack that palate of yours with more sweetness than you had when you were hammering back a gallon of soda and five packs of sour candies.

But if you get your sweetness from the right sources, you are going to be healthier, fitter, and happier. You will not run the risk of diabetes. Your brain will have the fuel that it needs to sustain a high level of concentration.

And believe me, experimenting with fruit is fun. There are at least several kinds of them out there for everybody. Find what yours are and every time you get the urge for sugar, use them.

Now, all this might be fine and good when it comes to stuff that is already in our homes. But what, you might ask, should we be doing when we hit the grocery store? How will we make sure we do not just cave and buy a bunch of sugary junk when we are surrounded by it?

Grocery Shopping While Craving Sugar

Maybe the best advice my mom ever gave me was never to go grocery shopping on an empty stomach. She told me that what would happen was I would wind up buying to satisfy my hunger, without thinking long-term. I would wind up, she said, with a bunch of junk, and only have to go back a second time to get all the healthy stuff I needed.

Being young, though, I did not listen. In fact, it took me a few tries before I finally learned the wisdom in this piece of advice. Until then, I would just shove whatever looked good at the time into the cart, forgetting that I would need essentials.

Now, I heed this advice 100% of the time. Why? Because it is sensible. You need to shop with your head, not your stomach. You need to think about your purchases, look at the ingredients, and weigh the prices—the works.

With sugar, of course, this becomes a little more challenging. Because, as we discussed earlier, being around sugary foods can trigger the urge to eat them. And grocery stores really do have wonderful displays of unhealthy foods, particularly in the pastry section.

(For me, there is an aesthetic value to the doughnut that I think comes from both the grocery store and *The Simpsons*. So, I get it.)

What, then, are we supposed to do when we enter the grocery store and wind up in the throes of a deep-seated sugar craving?

First, let's pull back a bit to the advice my mom gave me. Since the goal here is to avoid sugar, we need to begin shopping by doing so with our heads, not our stomachs. Coming up with a grocery list is advisable, of course, because you can make sure you stick to it and refuse to buy anything else. But also thinking about avoiding certain sections altogether could help! Maybe just stay in meat and produce, grab a loaf of bread, and get the heck out of there while the going's good.

This is, of course, much better than entering the grocery store with no plan and impulse-buying whatever catches our eye. But it still does not answer the question of what to do when we encounter sugary foods and drinks and develop a craving.

And look, I wish there was an easy answer here. I wish there was some method where you could close your eyes and think of England, and the craving would disappear in a puff of smoke.

But there is no such method. All you have, frankly, is your gumption.

But this is not nothing! You, as a human being, are filled with the stuff—gumption, I mean. You have more than enough willpower to get you through encountering sugar in the wild.

You really don't have to buy sugary things any more than you have to eat them. This is a choice you get to make, one way or the other.

And, of course, there is still mindfulness to use. But even being good at mindfulness does not mean that the urge to buy sugar will not arise. It most certainly will, so long as you are in the presence of sugary foods. And, alas, there is really nothing you can do about it.

What this means, then, is that when you go to the grocery store, you are encountering a test. Now, this is not a bad thing—in fact, it is a good thing. It means that, having put in all that legwork to get you doing well at home, you now get to see how much it has paid off out in the wild.

Look, I could go on here about how adversity makes us stronger, yada yada... And that is true, don't get me wrong. But there is no denying that doing something like this is genuinely challenging. And really, my heart goes out to you.

But the fact of the matter is that unless you plan on staying in your room for the rest of your life, this is something you have to learn how to handle. And believe me, the more you do it, the easier it gets. Denying yourself unhealthy food becomes a habit in itself. And once that happens, you are golden.

This reminds me of something I heard once.

A priest is sitting in a confessional booth, when all of a sudden a man bursts in, ready to make a confession.

"Father," the man says, "I have to tell you. Last night I was out boozing downtown. And I met the most beautiful woman I've ever seen. She flirted with me all night, Father, and then she asked me to go back to her place with her."

"I see," says the priest. "And did you?"

"Why, of course! But then, get this: When I got back, her roommate was there. Maybe even more beautiful than she was! Anyway, the two of them got talking, and they thought maybe the evening should involve the three of us, if you catch my drift."

"Oh dear," says the priest. "And did you succumb to temptation, my son?"

"Yes, Father, I did. And I tell you, once it was through, I came straight here."

"This is a grave matter. I'll ask that you say 30 Hail Marys—"

"Hold up, Father," the man says. "I should stop you there. See, I'm not Catholic."

The priest is surprised. "You're not Catholic? Then why did you tell me all this?"

"Are you kidding?" the man says. "I'm telling everybody!"

Okay, yes, this is a good joke. (If you disagree, then something is wrong with you far worse than the sugar addiction.) But what can we learn from this joke, if anything? Is it simply some comic relief in the midst of things getting a little too serious there for a second?

Our relationship to temptations is interesting. Even when we know things are bad for us, and even oftentimes *because* they are bad for us, we have a strong desire to do them anyway. And, what's more, we tend to enjoy them. A lot.

Most people I think would say that the guy in the joke really did not transgress a significant boundary. At least, most people in the West, anyway. But I think we all recognize the gleefulness with which he indulges in what, to the priest, is a grave sin. We recognize it as something in ourselves, something crucial to the human condition.

I know, I am getting a little deep here. But guess what? We are talking about something that has real depth. We are talking about our relationship with things that are bad for us and how we can order our lives against overindulging in them.

A sugar habit does produce pleasurable feelings, of course. But so does transgressing the prohibition against eating sugar. It makes doing it feel *bad*, in a cool way. You know it does because transgressing against all kinds of prohibitions produces the same result.

Anyway, not to get too heady here, but this is what we are up against. So, when we go into the grocery store, even if and when we have a plan to keep ourselves away from the doughnuts, the doughnuts will still be there. And no matter how much fun getting them would be, no matter the thrill of doing something wrong, we have to ready ourselves to stay away from them, keep on track, and continue the trend toward healthy living.

***

Okay, that about sums up how to use food to stay away from sugar. And I think we have a decent idea now of what to do when we enter a grocery store, and even before we enter it.

But what we started getting into with the grocery store is not specific to that location. What I mean is, the temptations are everywhere. You will find them in all manner of social settings, from dinner parties to birthday parties, even when just going out for food with your friends or family.

How to handle these types of situations is not always clear. Oftentimes, in fact, it's quite murky. There are weird issues of politeness and so forth that come up, a strange fear over whether or not we are making people uncomfortable by not ordering dessert. Or, even worse, a fear of whether they will somehow look down on us for not indulging.

But whether or not that is only in our heads (it is) we need to have the skills ready to handle those situations. Because they will come up, without a doubt. And we need to know what to do when that happens.

Stay with me then, and we will learn how to navigate the opaque waters of fighting temptation in a social setting.

Chapter 6:

Handling Social and Emotional

Challenges

When dealing with some type of food-related problem, it would, of course, be easiest if we never had to leave the house. Even with something like counting calories. If we stay home, we are surrounded by the things we choose to surround ourselves with. We have a fridge packed with fruits and vegetables, we have crackers for a snack, and not a bag of chips in sight.

Now, this is much more challenging when it comes to sugar addiction. Any type of eating-related pathology comes with similar pitfalls and difficulties, but when in the throes of an addiction, this is only amplified.

The fact of the matter is, we have to go outside at some point. Really. We have to visit friends or family, or go out to eat every now and again. We can't just cordon ourselves off from temptation, in other words. Which means we need to build up the type of skills and resilience which allow us to do this without falling off the wagon.

Here, we are going to get into some of the strategies we can use to pull this off. They are not foolproof. They are not "plug and play," as they say. Some of them may work for some of us, but others will have no effect at all. It is up to us to figure out which ones work and pivot away from the ones that do not.

But first, let me tell you a story.

When I was a kid, my dad was going through what would become his final attempt at quitting smoking. He'd started smoking before he was even a teenager. It had been a part of his life for so long that he almost did not know what kind of man he'd be without it. In other words, smoking was a significant part of his personality.

By the time I was around 12, he had tried quitting about a dozen times. And he had tried every way he could, from the gum to the patch, to hypnotism and therapy and a few others. Finally, he had decided that the only way through was with his willpower. And that was what he decided to do.

He told all of us that it was coming. He set a date. He said, "October 9th is my first day. And the first three days are essential. I don't want anything around me that makes me wanna smoke. You understand? That means I need you guys to be patient. And I need you guys to try and give me some room. I wanna get this done but if I'm gonna pull it off, we'll need to do it as a family. Everyone cool with that?"

Of course we were. We wanted the old man to get healthy and stay away from smoking. And if that meant giving him a lift, then so be it.

We all worked together just as he asked. We gave him his space. When he got snippy and mad, we let it slide and reminded ourselves it would be over soon. And after about two weeks of this, when he seemed to be coming through the other side, he gave us all a big hug and apologized for how he had been. He even took us out for ice cream.

The only problem was, he had learned the wrong lesson from that whole experience. Because, while he continued to not smoke, he understood that his family helping him out was a big part of how he managed that. Which, to him, suggested that everyone around him was responsible for keeping him away from cigarettes. And that they were the ones who had to change—not him.

Just as an example: We had a wedding for my aunt about six months after Dad's quit date. It was a big wedding because my aunt's fiancée had a huge family. And there was talk, of course, about Dad's plan for staying away from cigarettes. How he should not drink too much, because losing his inhibitions was likely to result in him smoking. How if he felt like he needed one, he could leave at any time and go for a walk without any questions asked. And, furthermore, that if he needed to leave entirely, then Mom was to give him a pass, no matter how important his being there was.

In other words, him not smoking was the priority. Which was just fine by us.

The only thing was, a bunch of my cousins and a few of my uncles did what men tend to do at weddings, and

treated it as an occasion to smoke cigars. They would go to this little area just outside the venue and stand around and smoke stogies together, usually with a glass of whiskey in hand. And even though the smoking area was located far enough away from the entrance to reduce secondhand smoke, of course, there was the smell to contend with. And, obviously, the sight of them smoking.

Which was not an issue for most people. But for my dad it was.

I knew when we first saw them that he was going to be bothered by it. I saw it on his face as we were walking in, how he shook his head and grumbled something. I did not make out quite what he said, but I knew it had some words in it I was not allowed to use.

"What's the matter with them?" he said to my mom. "Out here, smoking."

"It's their choice," Mom said. "Just don't worry about them. We'll go inside and get a table."

"It's the *smell*. You smell it? Disgusting."

"I know. Filthy habit."

We took our seats for the reception which I remember was fun and romantic and all those things a wedding reception should be. But my dad, frankly, was spoiling the whole thing.

He kept shaking his head, rubbing the outsides of his hands. He turned to my mom and said, "How come nobody told them?"

"Told them what?" Mom said.

"Don't they know I'm trying to quit? Christ, you can smell the cigars all the way in here."

"I can't smell anything."

"Well, I can. I have a sensitivity. Seeing as I just quit."

"They're allowed to do what they want. It's their lives."

He shook his head. "Somebody should have told them. Inconsiderate, that's what they are. Only care about themselves. Even then, they don't care about themselves enough to stay healthy, do they? No, no. They're gonna wind up with mouth cancer. All because they were too inconsiderate. Bothering people. Bothering *me*."

This went on for long enough that my mom started to get mad at him. She told him to calm down, which, frankly, was not the best idea anyone had ever had. Because he finally lost control of himself, stood up with a shot and said, "That's it! If no one's gonna do anything about this, I will!"

We tried to stop him. Really, we did. But we did not want to make a scene either, so Mom and I had to follow behind him, whispering for him not to do this, while he just ignored us and marched right outside.

Everyone who was smoking a cigar was there all at the same time. They were laughing too, I remember. And one by one, they noticed my dad's expression and one by one, they all grew worried and confused.

"Something wrong?" one of them said.

"Wrong!?" Dad could hardly contain himself. "You have no consideration for others! You stand out here with your, your *stogies*, and you puff away and you puff and—you have no consideration! Who knows if somebody doesn't like the smell or even likes to *see* people smoke? You ever think of that? Huh? And what about—what about someone who's trying to *quit*, eh? No, you never thought about that. All you ever think of is yourselves!"

Here, my Uncle Vernon spoke up. He was older, grizzled. He had lived a hard life, hung out in bars, that sort of thing. He had an enormous stogie between his teeth and was never intimidated by anybody.

So, when he stepped through the crowd of cigar-smokers, everyone took notice. A hush, as they say, fell over the crowd.

Uncle Vernon looked my dad right in the eye. And he said, "Who cares?"

For a second, I wondered if my dad was about to really blow his top. But he had been so wound up there was nowhere else for him to go. It wasn't like he could be angrier, is what I mean. So, with my mom holding onto his arm, he said, "We're going home." And all of us got our things together and left.

Now, it took some time for my dad to see the wisdom in what Uncle Vernon had said. In fact, he took Uncle Vernon's response to mean that, as Dad had suspected, Uncle Vernon really did not care about anyone but himself. That if he was bothering people, that was just fine by him.

But there was something much more intelligent that I think Uncle Vernon was getting at. See, my dad was suggesting that all those men should make their decisions solely based on the whims of other people. He was saying that since he was having trouble with smoking, it was everyone else's job to take care of him.

If someone wanted to smoke, in other words, they would have to put that desire on hold while my dad was around. Because his needs came first.

Now, I am not suggesting that my dad was wrong about them smoking cigars. Cigars are certainly bad for you. And if you do indulge in them, it is always best to do so away from others. Most people find the habit disgusting and do not like the smell, at the very least.

But they are also their own people, with their own wants and needs, and their own choices to make. It was not their duty to make sure nobody would be made uncomfortable by their choices. They were not tempting my dad to continue smoking. They were doing their own thing.

It was my dad who needed to change. He needed to recognize that he had no control over the choices of others. That other people did not hold him in such high regard that they were willing to cater their personal choices to his needs.

At this point in time, my dad recognizes this. He has since apologized to everyone whom he yelled at that day. Which is nice! But what it took, I think, was more times where he went out into the world, encountered a smoker and grumbled, or was passive-aggressive toward them. He would come out of a hotel, see a smoker, and say to my mom, "Nice people are so considerate about smoking these days." Of course, loud enough that the smoker could hear it.

Because really, how many times can you do that before you realize you have not gotten people to stop doing things around you that you do not like? He was always going to encounter tobacco in the wild. He will continue to do so for as long as he is alive, I am sure.

The only thing he could change was his own self. He could come up with his own coping mechanisms for when he felt the pull of temptation.

And that was all. And now that he has done that, he is much happier, feels way less stress, and is much less reluctant to get outside and do things. Because he knows how to keep himself cool when he is around cigarette smoking.

The point here is that you can't convince other people that your eating habits are their business. It is not their job to make choices with you and your sugar issue in mind.

What you need to accept is that this is out of your control. But what actually is in your control is how you react to it.

How to Handle Cravings in Social Settings

We have already hinted at what I think is the most important thing here. But I think it is worth zeroing in on because all things related to this subject flow from this one principle.

And which one is that? Well, it's simple: You only have control over yourself. Not of your environment, and certainly not of other people.

Some people really struggle with this. I have already hinted that my dad had issues related to control. But even among friends, I have known more than a few who have been dictatorial, who have insisted that they act as a kind of policeman when it came to other people's behavior.

This really is not the best way to go about anything. Because not only does it alienate people, but it just flat-out does not work.

Let's start with the idea that it alienates people. The fact is, people really do not like being controlled by others. I know, shocker. But especially among friends, if people feel like someone has taken on a policeman-like role, people will inevitably get their backs up and wind up rebelling.

Don't believe me? Think about what would happen if, say, one of your friends went vegan. We have all had at least one, or even been one ourselves, so it should not be hard to imagine.

Imagine on the one hand that your vegan friend, every time they went out with you, made private decisions regarding what they would eat—say, ordered a vegan dish, or made sure their cocktail did not have egg whites in it. There was no production made about it, and while they were willing to discuss their dietary choices, they really only did so when asked.

This is a pleasant person. But now, let's imagine another scenario.

In this one, your friend has gone vegan. But when they come out to dinner, they make a big deal about not eating meat or dairy. They scold the waitress for working in a place that provides meat and dairy options, and then insist they watch a whole bunch of documentaries so they can see the level of genocide that they are complicit in.

When that is over, your friend turns to all of you and insists that while they are around, none of you can eat meat or dairy. It makes them too sensitive when they think about all the poor animals. They say something like, "You can make whatever decisions you want, I guess, but when you're around me, don't eat that garbage."

And *then*, when someone speaks up and says, "Hey man, maybe not all of us are vegans…?"

Well, you can imagine what happens next. Your friend goes into a tirade, insisting that the one who spoke up is a psychopath. That they lack the common decency to make even one small change.

Finally, your friend insists that if you do not all go vegan, they will not be friends with you anymore. Your friendship is conditioned upon your shared dietary choices.

Okay, so—this is not meant to pick on vegans. I chose them because I think we have all known at least one who has acted in the latter sense. When people get onto a new kick, they really do become evangelists for a spell, don't they?

The thing is, you can sub out "vegan" for lots of other things. More so than drawing attention to whatever choices that person has made, the point I am trying to make is this: How long would you let someone treat you this way before you decided not to hang out with them anymore?

Whatever your answer is, if you are being honest with yourself, I am sure there is a limit. And whatever that limit is, just know that other people have a limit too. And if you treat them in this way, you are running the risk of pushing them over theirs.

In other words, as you enter into a period of not eating sugar, it is improper, I would argue, to make this choice the business of others. Other people are not there to do what you want them to. The choice not to eat sugar was yours, and yours alone. And so, alas, you more or less have to do this by yourself.

This, then, means you need to try things like mindfulness in order to push through times when everyone around you orders dessert. Or you need to find an excuse and duck out early if you feel like you are about to cave. Whatever the case may be, you need to put mental or physical distance between yourself and the object you are trying to stay away from.

But, I am going to argue, the most important thing is…

Developing Resilience

Look, I'm not judging. But we do live in an age where resilience is, at the very least, not actively encouraged. And not that our current priorities are necessarily bad either. There is a reason why we have leaned into being more expressive, taking better care of one another, letting our emotions hang out on our sleeve—that sort of thing. And it is because for too long, we have pushed those feelings down and, likely, done serious psychological harm to ourselves in the process.

But.

This cultural emphasis is not, like everything, without its drawbacks. And one of those, I think, is a general lack of resilience among people.

Whether or not that is quantifiable I will leave up to people whose job it is to know things like that. For me, I will only say that resilience comes from making a habit of confronting things that are challenging. And whether or not I am right that the ability to confront challenges is on the decline, this is nonetheless how resilience is built up, and is what we should be using to confront sugar-based challenges in the real world.

What I mean here is that you have to actually go out and experience those challenges firsthand. Maybe for you, this is like a cold pond and you have to enter it slowly so you can get used to it. Maybe you prefer to just dive in and let nature do its work. Whatever it is, you need to get in there at some point, or you will forever be the person shivering at the edge of the water while everyone else is splashing each other, laughing and having fun.

Unfortunately, the only way to do this is to actually get on out there and face the sugar. You have to be willing to go out into environments where other people are going to be eating dessert and drinking soda, and you have to deal with your temptations privately. And furthermore, you have to do this enough times that it becomes a habit. Once it is a habit, you are on the right track. But there is only one way to make a habit, and that is all there is to it.

Now, this should not sound negative or discouraging. I think it is a bit of a harsh reality, but as a human being, this is something you are capable of doing. Not everyone is capable of everything, but through the history of our species, plenty of wild and incredible things have been done.

Whatever else you might be or become, this is absolutely in your wheelhouse. So, have courage, be confident, and get out there.

It will only get easier with time. I promise.

***

I hope by now it is clear what you need to do to manage cravings in public. I hope that it is clear also that the world outside of your comfort zone is unavoidable, but that it is character-building to encounter it with strength, to build resilience.

The only question now is—does any of this stuff actually work? What might it look like when applied to the real world?

With that question in mind, I think we should look at some stories about doing just that and see if maybe we can apply some of the lessons in them to our own lives.

Chapter 7:

Motivation and Persistence

The purpose of this chapter is to use narrative to our advantage.

What does that mean? Well, I have kind of an old-school approach to hearing stories, or reading stories, or however I wind up consuming them. See, way back in the olden times, people read stories in order to look for exemplary figures they could model themselves after. Greeks did this with Achilles, for example, and Romans did this with Aeneas. Beyond fiction, people do this today when, in the United States, we tell stories about George Washington.

So here, I am going to provide you with some stories about meeting the challenge of overcoming sugar addiction in the wild. And the purpose of this is to possibly show us the way to doing it ourselves. These are people we can model ourselves after, using the lessons they learned, and whatever else we can glean from the text.

I hope you find them useful. So, with that, here they are:

Martin's Story

So, my story, I guess, starts when I was a little kid. My parents never really got along super well, and there was always fighting in the house. We didn't live in a very big house either, so every time they fought, my sister and I could hear everything.

Sometimes, it would get so bad that my dad would leave for a week or more. I don't know where he went. Even to this day, I've never asked him. Although I've heard like, rumors and stuff. But I never believed those. Or I tried not to, anyway.

What would happen is, my mom would feel bad that my sister and I knew what was going on. And we were obviously stressed because my sister got alopecia when she was young. So, what my mom would do is take us to the store and let us buy sugary snacks. Whatever we wanted, one bag each. And we'd all three of us sit in the car and eat them. All things considered, it was kind of a pleasant experience.

The only thing is, I got to thinking of food as comfort. Like it was there to make me emotionally stable. And, specifically, it was that way with sugar.

So, as I grew older, I relied more and more on candies to get me through my day. I have a lot of stress, like ambient stress. As you can imagine. And I'll get into this later, where I think it was coming from. But mostly, yeah, ambient stress, so I'd always walk around with bags of candies and just kinda eat them throughout the day.

I never thought of what I was doing as serious. Or even as an addiction. Like, I'd see people in high school, students and whatever, and they'd be smoking. And I'd think that was so gross, that someone could get addicted to smoking.

What I didn't know was, you know, that I was doing all kinds of damage to my own body. I was way overweight, for starters. I'd get cranky if I didn't have my sugar. And I was spending a pretty significant amount of money on plastic bags of candy.

As I grew older, I never went to college. But I did get a job in a factory. And I'd always have a bag of candy on me. Usually a few, anyway, since I ran out so many times in a day. It was always just kinda there, like I'd get a negative thought about something, plop in a candy, and boom—the negative thought would go away.

I think I can swing back around to that thing I flagged earlier, about having ambient stress and stuff. So, like, I definitely did have that. And some of that, for sure, comes from my home life. But I gotta wonder, is it not possible that the sugar was creating the problem it was trying to solve?

Know what I mean? Like, how much of feeling bad was because I was shoving that much sugar into my body?

I dunno, I think probably lots, to be honest with you. Because eventually, yeah, I got diabetes and stuff. And the doctor told me it was because of all that sugar and I just thought that was nuts. At the time, anyway. I was like, "Are you kidding me? This isn't even that much. My sister is way worse than I am."

And she was. No doubt. She went off to college because she was the smart one. So, she was away for a few months until reading week. And when she came back, I hadn't seen her in the longest stretch of my life. And she was way more overweight than she'd been the last time I saw her.

That girl also drank a lot of sodas, which didn't help. No, that didn't help at all.

The thing was, of course, she also got diabetes. Right after I did, she got diagnosed. So, we had to come up with a plan for the two of us, because diabetes ain't fun, I promise you. And to our credit, we knew right away that this was a sign we had to stop things. Maybe it wasn't rock bottom, but it sure didn't feel good.

The two of us committed to cutting the refined sugar out of our diet. And it was *hard*. We had to do it gradually, too, since we both ate so damn much of the stuff. And the only reason we knew that was because we tried cold turkey and each of us felt like we were gonna have a damn seizure.

So, we cut ourselves off a little at a time. And to compensate for what we weren't eating, we had the bright idea that maybe we should try fruit. I know, seems like such a no-brainer. But at the time, well, I'm kind of embarrassed to say, but I couldn't remember the last time I'd had any. Unless potatoes counted, but I don't think they do.

Alright, so here's the thing I learned about fruit. When you're used to eating candies all day—like the gummy, plastic bag-candies—fruit does not taste sweet *at all*. It tastes pretty plain. Like what I imagine a carrot tastes like to most people. So, right away, I tried apples. And I was like, "The hell is this? How am I supposed to eat something that tastes like nothing at all?"

In fact, I almost gave up on eating fruit altogether. But my sister said someone had told her that eventually I'd get used to it. And she didn't like it either but maybe we just had to power through and hope for the best.

I thought that was a bunch of nonsense. But I figured it was worth a try. And so, the more I cut down on candies, the more I added fruit into the mix. And what happened was, I started throwing in like, raspberries and blackberries. All kinds of stuff. And I really started to like them.

Eventually, I got to where I'd cut refined sugars out completely. But I swear, I eat more fruit than anyone you've ever met. And I feel *great*. The diabetes has gone into remission. I've lost a whole bunch of weight.

Do I slip up every now and then? Of course. This is what happens though, you know? We all slip up. But it's part of the story of recovery, so if it happens to you, just pick yourself back up and start again.

The real trick I've found, though? I know I was using refined sugar to cover up my emotions. I know they were causing a bunch of my bad emotions too, but I know the way I grew up left a mark on me.

Getting rid of refined sugar has left me space to deal with that. So, now I get to face reality every day and I get to be stronger and grow as a person.

Believe me, if I can do this, you can too.

Jacqueline's Story

I wanna tell you about the first time I went out to a dinner party after quitting sugar.

It was sort of a long process for me, getting away from the stuff. I was always known sort of as the "fat girl," or at least that's what I imagined everyone thought. I can be a bit self-conscious and I admit that.

So, as you can imagine, I didn't like standing out for being overweight. Or that, you know, I was overweight and my friends weren't. Because I imagined that made me stand out. And I just wanted to stay under the radar, so I made the commitment to quitting sugar. And it took some doing, but eventually, I got to where I was happy with my weight and I wasn't eating the stuff. And everything was good!

The only thing is, I'd basically locked myself inside to do it. I've worked from home since the COVID-19 pandemic, which was good for this whole process. But it's not sustainable either. I was single at the time and I didn't really like being alone, which meant I'd have to go out at some point.

Yikes, I can be such a mess.

Anyway, what happened was, I got invited to my friend Denise's because she was having a dinner party and what have you. Not for anything special; we'd just all been inside from lockdowns and stuff, and we needed to get out and stretch our legs. It just seemed like a fun thing to do.

And yeah, I was all excited to show off how I'd lost 40 pounds in six months. (Can you believe that!?) But I also knew this was gonna be a serious danger zone. Because like, my friends are all skinny, but they do still like to eat desserts and drink cocktails.

Okay, so here's what I did. I went in prepared, which I think is always a good idea. I had a plan, I knew what was gonna be for dinner, and I knew that it was healthy. But I also knew there'd be snacks and dessert and that if I didn't show up with my own drinks, I'd wind up having a bunch of sugary things shoved in my face. Not because my friends are inconsiderate or anything, but just because it wouldn't occur to them that maybe those were things I can't drink.

I brought gin and soda. It just seemed like that was a low-calorie thing to drink. It's pretty low in sugar because soda is just water. And gin, well, it's not the sweetest thing in the world anyway.

So, I figured I was at least making a decent step in that direction. And then, yeah, I showed up after giving myself a big pep talk and whatever, and I was nervous, but I went anyway.

For the most part, everything was fine. There were like, seven or eight of us there. We had these big, beautiful salads, and I drank my gin while the girls drank their white wines and their fruity cocktails. We had a blast.

And by the way, every one of them said how I'd lost weight. This kinda defeated the whole purpose of not wanting to stand out, but I guess if I'm gonna stand out for anything, that's a good one. Right? And anyway, it wouldn't be long before that just became who I was and they stopped mentioning it. So, I was thinking long-term.

But then, of course, Denise came out with the cake and pie and ice cream. And I have to tell you, I *hated* the expressions on their faces. *Hated.* They were so happy and excited to have these things that they were gonna eat and they were all clapping and saying how beautiful they looked. And it made me so mad. It was like watching my friends cheer on a homicide or something. I could have killed them.

So yeah, they passed the cake and whatever else around and started eating. And all I can hear is the clanking sound their forks made against the plates, the moans and groans and "Ohmagod, this *SO GOOD*" that they all have as a prerecorded response.

I was ready to lose my mind. There was a horrible feeling that welled up in my stomach. And there was a pressure behind my eyes and I realized I was like, gripping the chair arms? Like real tight, I mean.

And then one of my friends, Dani, turned to me. And by the way, I like Dani. She's cool. And we're still friends. But obviously, she offered me cake and ice cream on reflex without thinking that maybe that would drive me bananas.

She held out a plate and said, "Want some?"

And I swear to you, I could have swatted that plate right into her lap. I saw the whole thing, how mad I was gonna get. It'd be like reality TV, with me throwing things and screaming and making a huge ass of myself.

Somehow though, I managed to just smile and say, "No, thank you."

It was the best I could do. Dani thought something was maybe up though; I could see it in her eyes. She set the plate down and I left for the washroom without telling anyone where I was going. Because I could feel anger and desire all well up into one big, like, *tornado*.

Once in there, I turned on the lights. I looked myself in the mirror. And by the way, I looked like trash. I could see how sweaty I was, how much I was shaking. It was crazy!

And I figured maybe I should just leave. I had way too big a problem with sugary foods to just hang around while everyone else ate. Maybe I just wasn't ready and I needed more time, or I needed to, I dunno, find new friends or a support group or something.

But then there was this huge part of me that thought like—why should I leave? Everyone else was having fun. They were my friends. So what if they were eating things I couldn't?

What did any of that matter?

All of a sudden, I got this huge confidence boost. I looked at myself and thought, yeah, I'm kind of a badass. I can totally do this.

And I went back out there, took my seat, and just let myself slide into the conversation. I had a few drinks, told a few stories… And by the end of the night, not only had I not eaten anything sugary, but I felt really, really good about myself for not doing so.

I'm not gonna lie and say it isn't still hard sometimes. Because it totally is. But after getting through that first one, I knew it would never be that hard again. And I was totally right.

Seriously. Just get through the first big one, and you'll be surprised at what you can accomplish.

***

Okay, let's take a pause here for a second.

So far, these two stories have been going over some things we have talked about already. Specifically, the process of getting off sugar in the first place, and then how to handle yourself when you finally go back out in public.

But there is one thing that we have not gotten into yet. And that is what to do if and when you have a relapse.

The sad truth about having an addiction is that the chances of relapse are always super high. I have known a few alcoholics in my time, and I have seen the pattern. They have gotten sober and been super high on their sobriety. Everyone who has talked to them has said later how wild it is that they seem so happy and well-adjusted.

But sooner or later, the old ways of thinking creep in. And you can tell they are starting to think about it. Just by the way they are telling stories about the times when they used to drink, or else they start rationalizing drinking as a coping mechanism. *Just for other people, you understand.*

Until it's not.

So yeah, once that kicks in, the route toward relapse is pretty well right in front of them. And more often than not, they slip on going to meetings, and then that's it: They drink one time, thinking this time they can handle it, and then they are back on the hooch.

(Sidebar: Is "hooch" not an excellent word?)

With that in mind, I think a story about relapsing with sugar would be beneficial. Because like it or not, if you have this problem, you are probably going to experience this. And maybe a little narrative about such a thing will help you to find inspiration.

So here it is...

Macy's Story

Getting off sugar was probably my proudest accomplishment. I've had a decent few of them also, which include working my way up to district manager at work, getting an MBA, and raising a few kids, all of whom turned out great. And I don't wanna give the impression that I'm downgrading my kids or whatever, just that I had such a bad sugar habit that it took me forever to get past it. Really, it took everything I had.

And by the way, I was off it for maybe five or six years. I told people how much I didn't miss it, how much I loved losing the weight, how I didn't wake up with the taste of something awful in my mouth. I was really invested in having gotten past refined sugar and caring for my health.

The only thing is, no matter what you do, it's not like life magically becomes super easy. It's easy for periods, and then it sucks. And when it sucks, it sucks big time.

What happened to me was my parents died within four months of each other. Mom had cancer, which snuck up on her and grew too quickly for her to fight it off. All in all, it took about two months for that process. And then four months later, after Dad was all lonely and really not handling it well, he had a heart attack while he was raking the leaves.

It was a lot to handle all at once. Becoming an orphan in my 50s, especially. I always thought I'd have longer. But, you know, I'm not in charge. I'm only a witness, like we all are.

Still, I took the whole thing pretty hard. My husband told me I was looking rough. And since I was doing a lot of my mourning privately, which meant he was only seeing a portion of what I was going through, that meant I was really in a bad place. I knew I needed to do something to stop myself from going overboard, I just wasn't sure what it was.

The first thing I tried was diving into work. I took on more projects than I normally do, worked twice the number of hours… Sometimes I even stayed over at the office. I slept under my desk. I made work my entire life, all to keep myself from having any downtime, since downtime meant thinking, and thinking meant despair.

You can imagine how this worked out. I was burning the candle at both ends. I was getting loopy and made a few dumb mistakes. A couple of them turned out to be pretty costly. And that was just at work—at home things were even worse. At one time, I hadn't seen my family, I realized, in three weeks.

Basically, all my despair was being offloaded onto other people. They were having to deal with the consequences of me not taking care of myself. At home, my family said I needed to be a part of their lives and that they were all worried about me. At work, there was a kind of intervention where I was told I had no choice but to take some time off.

I hated the idea of time off. I fought it as best I could. I insisted I'd hand off some of the projects to the other managers. I said that I'd cut back on the hours I was working and stop sleeping at the office. They said that wasn't good enough. They appreciated me making sure the work got done, but for my own health and safety, I needed to go home, deal with my [stuff], and come back when I was feeling well. Maybe see a therapist.

Well, needless to say, I didn't wanna see a therapist. As you can tell, I've never been the "confronting my demons" kind of gal. But I got my things together and went home and decided, alright, I'll give myself a few weeks, get the mourning out of the way, and then I'll get back to the job.

What I found, though, was that since my husband worked and the kids were either in school or with their friends, I actually had a lot of time to myself. Which, for most people, would probably be nice. But for me, this was a nightmare.

I had these recurring thoughts of my parents' suffering. How awful it must have been to be my dad after Mom died. Every time I had one of those thoughts, I did something to get the thought to shut up. Oftentimes, I'd pick up my phone to distract myself. But I grew conscious of this being a time suck and decided maybe it'd be best to watch TV.

And not like, trashy, distraction TV. I wanted to use my time wisely. Not have my brain turn to mashed potatoes. So, I watched documentaries, finally saw all of *Breaking Bad*, and even tried to get into foreign films, although some of them were beyond me.

All this took about two weeks. And I was getting antsy, bored. I was ready to go back to work.

Except, instead of talking to me directly, my boss called my husband to ask how I was doing. And my husband said I'd done nothing but veg out, watch TV. He said too—and this was probably true—that I was cranky, irritable. That I still looked sick from not sleeping. That instead of sleeping, I was just watching more TV.

I admit to all of that. How I found out this conversation had happened, though, was I called my boss and told him I was ready to come back. And he told me, no, he'd talked to my husband, yada yada... He said it sounded like I needed two more weeks off.

This was devastating to me. I was bored with the TV. I got into a fight with my husband over the whole thing and said he should mind his own business. He told me he was trying to help, I said this wasn't helping—you can imagine where this went.

Basically, I had no idea what to do. I could feel the lingering presence of my parents' deaths and I didn't want to feel that to the full extent. I was exhausted by mourning, even as I hadn't given myself over to it completely.

After two days of this, I decided to go for a walk and wound up in the convenience store. I had an idea I'd pick up some magazines and maybe some milk since we were running out. But I see now that my unconscious was calling the shots. I had no intention of buying either of those things. And I know this because the first thing I did was go to the soda fridge.

It was a strange feeling, looking in that fridge. They all sat there, the bottles and cans, with all those pretty colors. I knew which ones were my favorites from experimenting when I was young. And looking at them then, it was like I could taste them, which I know was a kind of hallucination, of course. But it was so powerful.

What happened then was, I think, what happens to most people with addictions of some sort or another. I had the following conversation with myself:

I'm not the person I used to be. Things are different now. The reason I had such a bad problem with them before was because I let them get the best of me. This time, I have the knowledge and experience to be in control of how much soda I drink. Because I know what it's like to drink too much soda and I won't let myself get there again.

Of course, I know I could just not drink them at all. But I did used to enjoy them. They made me feel good. And right now, I feel bad and there's just no way I can get back to work unless I give myself a bit of a jolt. Something to make myself feel good.

Yeah, that's it. This is a tool. I'm not using it as a crutch. I just need it to knock me out of this funk. And once I've done that, then I'll be fine, and I can give up the sodas again and everything will be fine.

I just need one. Or maybe a couple, but not many more than that. And then I'll feel better.

So, that's what I did. I bought three sodas, already going over what I said I was going to. And I walked around drinking them so nobody at home would see that I'd slipped.

When I was done drinking them, all three of them, I stood leaning against an old church. And I closed my eyes to take stock of my feelings. I wanted to see if the sodas had done the trick.

Remarkably, they had. I did feel much better than I had a few minutes ago. But, seeing as I have an addict's brain, the next thought I had wasn't that I should stop there like I said I would. It wasn't that the plan worked. I got a boost, and now was the time to get myself together with the help of all that sugar.

No, the next thought I had was: *Just think of how much better you'll feel if you have more.*

And I did have more, believe me. I spent the next week hiding them as best I could. But eventually, my husband found out, and he did his best to be supportive, but I could tell he was mad. And once the cat was out of the bag, I didn't feel the need to hide them anymore, so I just drank the sodas around the house. Nine or ten of them a day.

The kids saw I was back on the sugar. They were disappointed, I know, but they kept that to themselves. Which was nice.

At the time, I didn't really notice any of this—how it was affecting everyone else. I wound up with another two weeks off work, which by then was getting to be way too much. I was horrified at what was happening around me, so I just dove head-first into my old habits.

I ate like crazy. I drank like crazy. I felt bad, but in my mixed-up brain, that was almost a good thing. It was good that I felt bad, and I wanted, in a way, to feel even worse.

Eventually, my husband, God bless him, just broke. We were watching TV, and I had a big bag of chewy candies and a two-liter bottle of soda. And we weren't watching anything good, we were watching junk. And then, all of a sudden, he just turned off the TV, and he looked me right in the eyes, and he said:

"I can't watch this anymore."

"The TV?" But I knew what he was talking about.

"You need to get it together, Macy. I don't know what you need to do to get there, but you can't treat yourself like this. It's gotten out of hand."

He didn't say anything more either. He just turned the TV back on and laid back on the couch.

I could see in his eyes, though, that he wasn't watching the TV. He was thinking. He was trying not to, but he was. And he was thinking about how much I needed to change because it was hurting everyone around me.

I swear, that was what broke me. I suddenly looked around at myself and what I was doing. And I was more or less disgusted by it. I grabbed up the candies and the soda, went through the fridge and cupboard, and took out everything I'd been using to self-medicate. And I ran out to the garage and threw them all in the trash.

I didn't announce it to anyone, that I was done. But they all knew. And I knew they knew because the whole atmosphere around the house changed.

I wasn't weighing them down anymore.

Okay, let's get to the end here so I stop wasting your time. I can be so long-winded!

The long and the short of it is that I knew I had to let myself grieve. And that just as I'd done before I'd kicked the habit, I was using sugar to keep my feelings down. To solve this problem, I needed to be vulnerable in a way that I never had been before.

I let myself be vulnerable around my husband. Around my kids, well, I'm old school. I don't need my kids to see me like that. But my husband, that's different.

I let myself cry around him. I told him how lonely everything felt. How I couldn't stop thinking bad thoughts even when I tried not to. And you know what? He's a good man. So he was real supportive. He helped me a lot.

Eventually, I felt healed enough that I could get back to work. It was a bit of a slow process and everyone there was pretty tense, as though I might start overworking myself again. But gradually, we got through that and now I'm still at work and doing better than ever.

What's the lesson here? Well, I learned a few things. First, sugar addiction is as much a symptom as it is a problem in itself. We use it to mask certain things, especially thoughts we'd rather not have. Dealing with the underlying issues is the most important thing when it comes to dealing with problematic sugar eating. Believe me.

But the other thing is that we're still human. All of us. We're going to have thoughts we wish we didn't have, and we're going to rely, most of us, on unhealthy coping mechanisms when that happens. We're fallible, we're vulnerable, and we all do silly things from time to time.

For a while, during the relapse, I wondered if I was maybe just the weakest person ever—how had I let myself get to that place again? But I'm not. I'm just human. I have a monkey on my back, but we all do, in a way. And mine got the best of me for a spell. But in the end, I got the best of it.

That's the story of living, I think. So, if this happens to you, don't sweat it. Just pick yourself back up and get at it again.

***

Alright then, I think that should do it for the stories.

I hope they helped! I always find stories like these so inspiring, so I am guessing some of you may feel the same. There is no way I can be the only one, right?

That said, it is time to move on to what might be my favorite chapter in the whole book. Since here, we have gone over stories about recovery and relapse, of hope and perseverance, I think we next need to give some space to what happens to our bodies if and when we decide to kick the habit.

Just how healthy can we get by leaving refined sugar behind us? What happens to our physical selves when we do?

I think it's time to find out.

Chapter 8:

The Benefits of Breaking Free

From Sugar Addiction

Alright, we are approaching the end here. We have gone over, I think, most of the basics, and taken some deep dives along the way. By now, we should know what sugar addiction is, why it is harmful, and how we might go about dealing with one if we have to.

But maybe the most important question is: What happens if we *do* manage to throw refined sugar overboard? Why should we go through all the trouble of making new lifestyle choices, changing our eating habits, and possibly going through withdrawals? Are we actually going to see benefits?

What, in other words, is the point?

Well, I hope by the end of this chapter, you will agree that the health benefits are many. And more than that, I hope that this inspires you to seek these benefits out for yourself, if you are so inclined.

That said, here they are!

Weight Management

This is probably the biggest one when it comes to staying off the sugar. Obesity, as we all know, has become an enormous problem in the United States, not least of all because there are so many health problems that are downstream from it. Losing weight, then, is a great idea for your overall health, but also, for many people, for psychological reasons.

Anyone who has struggled with weight knows that it comes with a whole boatload of confidence issues. You become self-conscious in areas of your life where you never thought you would be. Like, say, going on dates. All of a sudden there is the problem of, "Is this person going to think I'm fat?", which is really stressful.

So, losing weight can help take some of that stress off, no doubt. It can make you feel more confident, make you want to go out more, and probably, as a result of this new confidence, make you appear more attractive to people. Not to say that people who are overweight are unattractive! I just mean that when you feel good about yourself, it tends to be contagious— other people feel good about you as well.

But coming back to the physical health effects: We have talked about how sugar intake is correlated with excess belly fat. And belly fat is the most dangerous of all, because of the strain it puts on your organs.

If you get off the refined sugar, or bring it down to below the recommended levels, you are likely to see improvements in this area, which means your chance of having a heart attack, for example, goes down.

So, chalk that up to one thing—a big thing—that can be improved by making healthier choices. And, given everything we just went over, it is a choice that creates a whole bunch of more positive health outcomes.

But that is not all! There is also…

Blood Sugar

This is an obvious one, but it is worth repeating. Blood sugar issues can spiral quickly into diabetes, and diabetes, while manageable, is not a desirable health outcome.

The list of side effects from diabetes, especially if it is not managed well, read almost like a horror novel. The most famous of these, to my knowledge, is that it can lead to dead tissue in the feet and legs, which can necessitate amputation. It is a bit of a stereotypical image, that of the diabetic with no legs, but it is a genuine possibility.

In fact, I remember one time I visited Thunder Bay, which is a major-ish city in Northern Ontario. Now, Thunder Bay is known as one of those cities where the gap between rich and poor is quite stark. There are some people who do quite well up there, but the level of poverty is among the worst in the whole country of Canada.

One of the most noticeable effects is seen in the Indigenous population. Largely due to the cycle of poverty, levels of alcohol abuse remain high in this subpopulation, which, due to the sugar content in alcohol, can lead to insulin problems, which results in diabetes.

The most obvious visual cue that diabetes is a major problem in Thunder Bay is, alas, the number of people who are wheelchair-bound due to a lack of lower limbs. It is a terrible sight, I promise you. But by all accounts, this is a problem of which many people in the city are aware.

Now, this is no place for political discourse, so I will leave the question of how this problem has arisen and how it might be dealt with for writers who know more about this area. For me, it is a reminder that not taking care of one's diabetes, or not being able to, can have permanent consequences.

Obviously in this book, we are not dealing with the problems of poverty and alcoholism. But since we are dealing with the problem of refined sugar, the effects that refined sugar can have on our health are no better represented than in the worst-case scenario.

In other words, reducing your intake of refined sugar can help make sure that this is never a problem you have to deal with.

Alright, now what about…

Oral Health

I hinted at this earlier when, in one of the stories, I mentioned having a mouth that had a particularly evil smell to it.

Well, hyperbole aside, refined sugars do a lot of damage to your oral hygiene. They make your mouth a breeding ground for bacteria which, all things considered, you would probably rather keep away from your mouth.

These bacteria can lead to all sorts of problems, not the least of which is genuinely bad breath. By now, most of us are aware of the types of problems we can have by not taking care of our teeth, including cavities, gum disease, and so forth. What we eat is a big part of how we prevent these types of things from happening, but even then, taking care of our teeth requires us to be more proactive than that.

What I mean is, even if we stay away from refined sugar, we should still be flossing, brushing, and rinsing twice a day. I know, most of us probably do one of those things once a day. But oral hygiene is important!

I mean, have you ever seen someone who has really bad teeth? It is quite a sight. My heart goes out to them, but boy, do I ever not want to have that problem.

No, it is certainly much better to have pearly whites, if we can. And because of that, it is best to make sure we eat well, take care of our teeth, and try to reduce the risks of rot, cavities, gum disease, and everything else.

And speaking of problems it is best not to have...

Depression

Yeah, this is a big one.

Earlier in this book, we went into some of the psychological effects of sugar addiction. And while it should be said that there remains controversy over whether or not refined sugar is a cause of depression, it is nonetheless true that what we eat has an effect on our brains. Taking care of what we eat—and furthermore, taking care of our physical health—is only going to lead to a healthier psyche.

However, if you have depression—if you get, as Winston Churchill put it, "visits from the black dog"—then it should be said that cutting out sugar is not going to cure you of the disease. Depression is a complicated beast, which has its roots in a number of neural systems, including various neurotransmitters. Treating it, therefore, is multifaceted, and often requires pharmaceutical as well as therapeutic interventions.

Meaning, that if you *do* have depression, you should not discount either of these options, pharmaceutical and therapeutic, as possible treatments. There will always be people who claim that there is a simple solution to depression, that it comes down to not getting enough sunlight, not listening to happy music, or not eating enough cucumbers or something. Alas, a simple solution to depression does not really exist, and you should, I will argue, be skeptical of claims to the contrary.

However, it is still true that our diets have an impact on our mental health. Eating a balanced diet, along with exercise, is one of the ways we can improve our mental health. And anyone who has had mental health problems will attest to this.

So, will cutting out refined sugar make the problem go away? Of course not. But there is a chance that it will make it better. And for that reason, it is possible that you can improve your sense of well-being by cutting out the sodas and candy.

And is that all? Not on your life. Because there is also…

Skin Health

You read that correctly!

Especially for younger people, acne can be a real pain. It is one of the monstrous transformations that comes along with puberty, where we are suddenly ashamed of every aspect of our bodies. For some of us, this can feel like the worst part of a David Cronenberg movie. For all of us, it is a strange time of drastic changes, in which we see the body become a different type of thing than what we had gotten used to.

Acne comes with a lot of baggage, considering it is one of the pubertal conditions that cannot be hidden. It is, after all, on our faces. The strange hairs we grow are hidden by clothes. And for men, the hairs they grow on their faces can be shaved off. (In fact, doing so is, for most young boys, a significant rite of passage.)

For girls, obviously, the changes regarding breasts are more conspicuous. But acne really draws a lot of attention to itself, and never, unlike breasts, in a positive way.

The writer Charles Bukowski had a great book about his early life called *Ham on Rye*. In it, he details his upbringing in as humorous a way as possible, but nonetheless describing events that would be traumatizing to anybody. This includes growing up under an abusive, tyrannical father and getting in near-constant fistfights.

And, crucially for us, a horrifying fight against acne and boils.

It is interesting that acne should make it into a book about the traumas of the man's youth. But for him, obviously, it held a privileged place in the hierarchy of traumas, particularly since it was so bad he had to get treated by doctors. The scarring on his face as an adult is at least in part due to his teenage acne.

My point is that having bad acne can be emotionally scarring and so trying to keep it at a minimum is something most people are interested in. In fact, I am 100% sure that nobody ever *wants* acne, although some people might have less of it and maybe be more laissez-faire about the whole thing.

Either way, cutting back on refined sugar can help keep breakouts down to a minimum. And so, in the interest of not having to endure the physical and psychological effects of this condition, cutting out added and refined sugars is a step in the right direction.

***

So, what can we say in summary?

What we put into our body, unsurprisingly, has an enormous effect on our body itself. Not just in the sense that we can gain weight either, although that is certainly part of it. No, what we put into our body affects everything from our skin health to our mental health and everything in between.

This, ultimately, means that being conscious of what we put into our bodies can have positive effects, which further means that cutting out refined sugars and kicking the addiction will pay dividends in many areas of your life.

It is possible to be fitter, happier, and healthier looking than what you look like caught in the maelstrom of sugar addiction. A better life, in other words, is on the other side of the decision to kick the habit.

Which, alas, brings us almost to a close here. Only one more stop and then we are through.

Conclusion

Addiction is a bit of a tricky subject, right?

On the one hand, we tend to think of it, understandably, as something that befalls substance abusers. We might think of movies like *Trainspotting*, or books like *Naked Lunch*. We think of alcoholics like Ernest Hemingway or Tennessee Williams. Or we might even be a little more expansive and admit that, yeah, it does go beyond substance and includes compulsive gamblers like Dostoevsky and Norm Macdonald.

But addiction *really* does include a lot of different things. Even if we are skittish about the word "addiction" and want to reserve it for substance and behavioral addictions, we can at least admit that our dopamine pathways can get us stuck in a cycle where we compulsively repeat behaviors or activities that are not to our benefit.

Do some people not get addicted to video games? Porn? Do some people get addicted to adrenaline, where they constantly seek out dangerous behaviors in order to get a kind of high?

Again, maybe the word "addiction" becomes too broad in this context. But there is at least a *kind* of addiction at play here. Something that is so *like* an addiction that it becomes virtually indistinguishable.

When it comes to sugar, this is really what we are talking about. We are talking about people who get a kind of high from consuming it, who then compulsively seek it out for that high, and then continue to use it for that purpose, even while it is having detrimental effects on their health.

And those effects, as we know now, are pretty severe. They include all manner of things from weight gain to heart problems to oral health problems, and possibly mental health problems.

People will continue to consume sugar even after they become diabetic. Even after they have gained over 100 pounds and have developed bad acne into their 30s. Even after they are having trouble sleeping and can't go a day without obsessing over the thought of having some.

To me, this sounds exactly like an addiction. Of course, I am not a specialist in this area. But even as a metaphor for that process, "addiction" seems like a pretty sound one to me.

But, God, it is unfortunate, isn't it? I mean, refined sugar is one of life's few pleasures. So, I totally get it. I understand completely why and how somebody winds up in this cycle. But the good things in life tend to be the ones that turn on us the hardest, and this is no exception.

The good news is, as I hope I have shown throughout this book, that if you are in the grips of a sugar addiction, it is totally possible to get yourself free. It is a formidable foe, but it is not unbeatable. With the right tools, you can throw it into the dustbin of your past and get on with living a happier, healthier life.

Maybe the stories I've included throughout this book have helped you realize that. Maybe they haven't. The point here was not to give direct, plug-and-play advice on how to navigate this. It was, instead, to show that it is *possible* to navigate. You can get through your addictions, you can kick them, you can move on.

And believe me, there are a gazillion ways to pull this off. Maybe you are the kind of person who can just go cold turkey, put it in the rearview, and move on. Maybe you are the kind of person who needs therapy or a doctor or some kind of support group. That is great too.

The point is not how you do this, so long as what you are doing is healthy. The point is that you do it *at all*. That you recognize how much better your life would be if you made this change. And from there, that you put a plan in place for making this happen.

This means you can no longer make excuses. It means you need to own your decisions and commit to making new ones. It means looking inward, seeing where you need to improve, and holding yourself accountable.

And guess what? This is totally doable. Remember when we talked about not making this decision anyone else's problem? We talked about that in the sense that quitting sugar should not inconvenience others. It should not become a burden to them. It is your burden and yours alone.

This also applies to the moment we realize our sugar eating has gotten out of control. Because no matter how many things we can think of that have driven us to this point, no matter which holes in our lives are being filled by sugar, we are the ones who made the decision. We decided to eat the cookies. Nobody else did.

Which is kind of a horrifying thought, right? *It is our fault that this happened.*

But do not let that be accusatory. If we think along these lines and it gets us down, then we have not thought this scenario through properly.

When we say that this is our fault, all we should mean is that we are taking responsibility for ourselves. Not that we *cannot* blame this on anything else, but that we *will not* blame this on anything else.

And in not blaming it on anything or anyone else, we know that other people will not make the opposite decision for us. *We* will make the decision to stop. *We* will make the decision to get healthy. And *we* will be the ones that pull it off.

Not that there will never be others there to help us. For most of us, there will, of course, be that. Family, friends, doctors, you name it.

But if it turned out tomorrow that there was not a soul in the world willing to help us, what would we do? Give up? Say it was too big a burden and just continue to indulge in the addiction? Or would we still own up to our responsibility and work toward becoming healthier and happier?

I hope it would be the latter. It *should* be the latter. Because the thing is, whatever problem we have that was filled with sugar, it does not detract from the absolute fact that our health is worth preserving. And the reason why it is worth preserving is because *we are worth preserving*.

We should not settle for feeling like junk. We should not settle for feeling crazy and sleep-deprived and having bad breath. In short, we should not settle for feeling bad about ourselves. We should not settle for feeling less than optimal as often as we possibly can.

So, you see—or at least I hope you do—that turning the blame inward is liberating. It does not beat us down. It does not make us feel like we are worthless. It shows us our own value. It lets us know that our decisions matter. And we know they matter because they have consequences, both good and bad.

Is getting off sugar a simple matter then? Of course not. It requires a deep probing into ourselves, let alone hours of effort, both physical and mental, to get ourselves to where we would like to be.

But are we capable of pulling it off? You bet we are. Because, at the end of the day, our decisions matter. And we matter.

Putting those two things together is, for my money, the ultimate recipe for success.

***

Well, the time to leave is at hand. But before we part ways, let me tell you one last story to end things.

At the beginning of this book, I told you about Ralph. Ralph, if you recall, was a notorious soda drinker. All over town, he was known for his poor dental hygiene, for his compulsive sugar consumption, and for being something of a menace as a result.

When I last told you about him, I said he was staring down the barrel of some pretty serious medical problems as a result of his habit. Diabetes was almost certainly in his future. And his teeth would likely all fall out, all things considered.

All of which was true. Except I left out the end.

See, Ralph eventually did have a pretty serious health scare. The details have been a bit hard to come by, but my understanding is that he had some kind of an episode where he passed out at a local bar. He was standing there, chugging back his orange soda, and then his eyes rolled into the back of his head, and he fell backward. Smacked his head right off the floor.

He had to go to the hospital, of course. And while there, the doctor told him that his health was in rough shape. That all this sugar was destroying his body and he needed to get it together or that was probably going to be the end of him.

Well, for some of us, it really does take the worst to teach us a lesson. I know in my own life that I have been educated by failure more than by success. And so, all told, Ralph had his wake-up call that day.

He got a hold of as many books as he could on the subject of sugar and what it was doing to him. He started seeing a counselor to work through some of his psychological issues.

And, lo and behold, within six months of his episode, Ralph was able to put sugar behind him.

I will not say there have not been some scars, so to speak. His teeth are still a mess. But he has lost weight. He seems happier, less spun out. Everyone I know who has run into him has spoken highly of his efforts to get himself healthy, for what would be the first time in his life.

Ralph, to this day, had maybe the worst sugar habit I have ever seen. But he got himself off the stuff and is living a better, happier life than he ever has before.

And if he can do it, I guarantee you can too.

Now turn the page for your exclusive bonus and let's get started with your sugar detox!

Your Exclusive Bonus!

Unlock Your Next Chapter: Take Your Sugar-Free Journey to New Heights!

As you close the final chapter of "Sugar Cravings Conquered," your journey towards a sugar-free life is just beginning. "Crush Sugar Cravings: Your Ultimate Detox Roadmap" awaits you as an exclusive bonus, propelling you towards sustained vibrancy, energy, and empowered choices.

How This Bonus Sets You Free:

This empowering bonus extends the tools and unwavering support found in the main book, guiding you towards a lasting victory over sugar cravings and embracing a life brimming with vitality. By scanning the QR code and accessing this bonus, you're taking the next powerful step towards enduring health and well-being.

Congratulations on your triumph over sugar cravings!

Scan the QR code to claim your exclusive bonus and ignite your journey towards a life free from the sway of sugar. We're thrilled to continue supporting you on this empowering path. Let this bonus be your companion as you realize the life of wellness and vitality you deserve.

Your Opinion Matters!

If "Sugar Cravings Conquered" has inspired and supported you on your journey to conquer sugar cravings, we would be honored to hear about your experience.

Your review can provide invaluable guidance and inspiration to others striving for well-being. Thank you for considering sharing your transformative journey with us.

With enduring encouragement and cheers to your vibrant journey,

Olivia Rivers

References

Holland, K. (2020, February 11). *The connection between sugar and depression.* Healthline; Healthline Media. https://www.healthline.com/health/depression/sugar-and-depression

Schaefer, A., & Yasin, K. (2023, May 30). *Experts agree: Sugar might be as addictive as cocaine.* Healthline; Healthline Media. https://www.healthline.com/health/food-nutrition/experts-is-sugar-addictive-drug

Westwater, M. L., Fletcher, P. C., & Ziauddeen, H. (2016). *Sugar addiction: the state of the science.* European Journal of Nutrition, 55(S2), 55–69. https://doi.org/10.1007/s00394-016-1229-6

Printed in Great Britain
by Amazon